THE BRITISH ACADEMY

CONSTANTINE THE GREAT
AND THE
CHRISTIAN CHURCH

BY

NORMAN H. BAYNES, F.B.A.

The Raleigh Lecture on History 1929

SECOND EDITION

WITH A PREFACE BY

HENRY CHADWICK, F.B.A.

LONDON
PUBLISHED FOR THE BRITISH ACADEMY
BY THE OXFORD UNIVERSITY PRESS

Oxford University Press, Ely House, London W. 1

GLASGOW NEW YORK TORONTO MELBOURNE WELLINGTON
CAPE TOWN IBADAN NAIROBI DAR ES SALAAM LUSAKA ADDIS ABABA
DELHI BOMBAY CALCUTTA MADRAS KARACHI LAHORE DACCA
KUALA LUMPUR SINGAPORE HONG KONG TOKYO

ISBN 0 19 725672 4

This Raleigh Lecture was first published in 1931 in volume XV of the *Proceedings of the British Academy*, pp. 341–442, and separately.

Reprinted 1934
Reprinted (with new preface) 1972

PRINTED IN GREAT BRITAIN

PREFACE TO THE SECOND EDITION

NORMAN BAYNES' Raleigh Lecture on Constantine provided not only a major and incisive contribution to the study of the subject, but also a unique survey of modern research to 1930, besides which almost all the subsequent bibliographical surveys have offered supplementary notes on narrowly defined areas within the field.[1] Since Baynes wrote, much good work has been done particularly on certain specific questions about which he said relatively little, such as the bearing on Constantine's religious allegiance of his coinage,[2] his legislation,[3] and the great foundations of his church buildings.[4] This has filled out many details in

[1] Good general surveys are given by A. Piganiol, *Historia* 1 (1950), pp. 82–96; K. F. Stroheker, *Saeculum* 3 (1952), pp. 654 ff.; G. Kretschmar, *Verkündigung und Forschung* (= Beihefte zu *Evangelische Theologie*) 13 (1968), Heft 1; J. Vogt, *Mullus, Festschrift Theodor Klauser* (1964), pp. 364–79.

[2] See M. R. Alföldi, *Die Constantinische Goldprägung* (1963), and P. M. Bruun's massive corpus of the coinage of Constantine and Licinius in the series *The Roman Imperial Coinage* VII (1966), edited by C. H. V. Sutherland and R. A. G. Carson.

[3] Cf. J. Vogt, 'Zur Frage des christlichen Einflusses auf die Gesetzgebung Konstantins des Grossen', *Festschrift L. Wenger* ii (1945), p. 118; J. Gaudemet, 'La législation religieuse de Constantin', *Revue de l'histoire de 'église de France* 33 (1947), p. 25. A. Ehrhardt argued that pagan clerks in Constantine's chancery were sometimes responsible for drafting legislation at variance with the emperor's intentions: 'Constantin d.Gr. Religionspolitik und Gesetzgebung', *Zeitschrift der Savigny-Stiftung für Rechtsgeschichte*, Rom.Abt.72 (1955), pp. 127–90; 'Some aspects of Constantine's legislation', *Studia Patristica* ii (Texte und Untersuchungen 64, 1957), pp. 114–21.

[4] See, for example, the relevant parts of the masterly survey by R. Krautheimer, 'The Constantinian Basilica', *Dumbarton Oaks Papers* 21 (1967), pp. 117–40, and L. Voelkl, *Die Kirchenstiftungen des Kaisers Konstantin im Lichte des römischen Sakralrechts* (Arbeitsgemeinschaft für Forschung des Landes Nordrhein-Westfalen, Geisteswissenschaften Heft 117, Köln/Opladen, 1964). On the Holy Sepulchre see E. Wistrand, *Konstantins Kirche am heiligen Grab in Jerusalem nach den ältesten literarischen Zeugnissen* (Acta Universitatis Gotoburgensis 58, 1952, 1), who insisted that Eusebius' account of the buildings presupposes that the Martyrium left the tomb-area open to the sky, and that the church of the Anastasis, clearly distinguished from the Martyrium by Egeria (*Peregrinatio* 48, etc.), was later than the Martyrium.
There is room for further investigation of the Constantinian endowments listed in the Life of Silvester in the *Liber Pontificalis*.
On the Arch of Constantine at Rome the classic study is now by H. P. L'Orange, *Der spätantike Bildschmuck des Konstantinsbogens* (1939).

the picture. On the other hand the general position occu-
pied by Baynes became the target of a frontal assault from
Henri Grégoire.[1]

Baynes and Grégoire radically disagreed in their estimate
of the credibility and in their judgement of the authenticity
of the Life of Constantine ascribed to Eusebius of Caesarea.
In a succession of papers from 1931 onwards Grégoire
urged and reiterated his opinion that the *Vita Constantini*,
while it may have some (hardly identifiable) kernel going
back to Eusebius himself, is in large part a later forgery
by a successor making use of Eusebius' *Ecclesiastical History*
but freely embroidering the story and farcing it with invented documents such as the 'absurd' letter of Constantine
to the Provincials on polytheism (*V.C.* ii. 24–42). The
purpose of the forger was to represent Constantine as a
Christian and his opponent Licinius as a pagan persecutor,
whereas in truth Licinius protected the Christians and Constantine was (like Porphyry) a pagan modernist, neutral as
between different cults. The entire story of Constantine's
conversion and vision is therefore, in Grégoire's view, a
tissue of lies and tendentious legend. Written at a time
when the Persian war had been abandoned, the author of
the *V.C.* wished to represent Constantine as a pacifist and
therefore invented the extraordinary letter to the Persian
king Sapor (iv. 9–13). The forger's confusion is shown by
his mis-dating of Maximian's death (i. 47)[2] after the death

---

[1] 'La "conversion" de Constantin', *Revue de l'Université de Bruxelles* 36 (1930–
1), pp. 231–72; 'La statue de Constantin et le signe de la croix', *L'antiquité
classique* 1 (1932), pp. 135–43; 'Eusèbe n'est pas l'auteur de la "Vita Constantini" dans sa forme actuelle et Constantin ne s'est pas "converti" en 312',
Byzantion 13 (1938), pp. 561–83; 'La vision de Constantin liquidée', *Byzantion*
13 (1939), pp. 341–51; 'L'authenticité et l'historicité de la "Vita Constantini"
attribuée à Eusèbe de Césarée', *Bulletin de l'Acad. Roy. Belg.*, Classe des Lettres
sér. 5, 39 (1953), pp. 462–79.

[2] In *Byz. Zeitschr.* 39 (1939), pp. 466–9, Baynes drew attention to the statement in *V.C.* i. 47 that after the death of Maximian 'others', related to him,
were also discovered conspiring against Constantine. Baynes suggested that
the chronological displacement of Maximian's death may have been caused by
some connection of thought with later events, viz. plots of other members of
Maximian's family which are otherwise unattested.

of Maxentius, and especially by his muddled account of Constantine's two wars with Licinius (i. 48–ii. 18), which not only seems to make the interval between them very short but also ascribes the first (not merely the second, as in Eusebius' *Church History*) to Licinius' persecution of the Christians and Constantine's crusade in their defence.

The hypothesis of a late fourth-century forger explained for Grégoire why the *V.C.* is not mentioned by or known to any fourth-century author, and is not even included in Jerome's catalogue of the writings of Eusebius.[1] The story of Constantine's vision is not mentioned by Cyril of Jerusalem, Rufinus, Gelasius of Caesarea, Ambrose, or Augustine.

Baynes remained unmoved by Grégoire's arguments, believing that his hypothesis created more problems than it solved and entirely failed to explain with what motive the alleged forger went to work: *cui bono?* His summary of Constantine in *Cambridge Ancient History* XII (1939) quietly ignored his principal critic (as Grégoire complained),[2] and he contented himself with three pages of reply in *Byzantinische Zeitschrift* 39 (1939), pp. 466–9, where among other arguments he makes the important distinction, confused in Grégoire's earlier articles, between the question of Eusebian authorship and the factual accuracy of his narrative. Baynes could make concessions on the latter but not on the former: 'The question is thus not whether the account given in the *V.C.* is historically accurate, but could Eusebius have written it?'

---

[1] Jerome, *de Viris inlustribus* 81. Jerome's silence is regarded as a weighty argument against Eusebian authorship by W. Seston, *Journal of Roman Studies* 37 (1947), p. 127, as well as by H. Grégoire. But Jerome's list of titles here, as elsewhere in this hasty work, is very incomplete. In any event, Jerome nowhere betrays special interest in Constantine. See a judicious discussion by F. Winkelmann, 'Zur Echtheitsfrage der Vita Constantini des Eusebios v. Caesarea', *Studii clasice* 3 (1962), pp. 405–12.

Paul Petit's attempt (*Historia* 1, 1950, pp. 562–82) to show that a draft of the *V.C.* was known to Libanius when he wrote *or.* 59 about 348–9, has not carried conviction against the criticisms of J. Moreau in *Historia* 4 (1955), pp. 234–45.

[2] *Byzantion* 14 (1939), p. 318.

In 1962 in a magistral survey Friedhelm Winkelmann summed up the critical problems which the *V.C.* presents and examined all the important modern literature on the subject.[1] His verdict goes against Grégoire and is in essentials sympathetic to the view formulated by Baynes. In the swing of opinion against Grégoire a decisive part has been played by the brilliant identification, made by A. H. M. Jones in 1951, of the verso of the London papyrus 878 as a roughly contemporary official copy of part of Constantine's letter to the Eastern Provincials (*V.C.* ii. 24–42),[2] one of the documents so vigorously derided by Grégoire and other sceptical scholars. The papyrus fragment corresponds to *V.C.* ii. 26–9 (Heikel, p. 52, 4–53, 16). Jones commented: 'The papyrus proves beyond all reasonable doubt the authenticity of one of the Constantinian documents cited by Eusebius in the *Life*, and implies that of the rest. It does not of course prove that the *Life* in which they are quoted is a work of Eusebius, but I find it difficult to

[1] 'Zur Geschichte des Authentizitätsproblem der Vita Constantini', *Klio* 40 (1962), pp. 187–243. See also F. Vittinghoff, 'Eusebius als Verfasser der Vita Constantini', *Rheinisches Museum*, N.F. 96 (1953), pp. 330–73.
Winkelmann, *Die Textbezeugung der Vita Constantini des Eusebius von Caesarea* (Texte und Untersuchungen 84, Berlin, 1962), is fundamental for the correction of Heikel's inadequate edition of the text. He has also studied Eusebius' low posthumous reputation (as Arian and Iconoclast), and the use of the *V.C.* from the fifth century onwards, in *Byzantinische Beiträge* (ed. J. Irmscher, Berlin, 1964), pp. 91–119.

[2] P. Lond. 878, briefly noticed by Kenyon and Bell in the *Catalogue of Greek Papyri in the British Museum* III (1907), p. xlii, was published in full by T. C. Skeat, 'Britain and the Papyri', *Aus Antike und Orient, Festschrift W. Schubart* (Leipzig, 1950), pp. 126–32. The recto contains part of a (certainly pagan) petition from the city of Arsinoe asking for tax relief. A. H. M. Jones, following a suggestion of C. E. Stevens that the *V.C.* would be worth looking at, identified the verso as Constantine's letter to the Provincials, and announced his discovery at the Oxford Patristic Conference in September 1951. His paper, with a re-edition of the verso of the papyrus by Skeat, was published in the *Journal of Ecclesiastical History* 5 (1954), pp. 196–200. The importance of the identification was underlined by Kurt Aland, 'Eine Wende in der Konstantin-Forschung?', *Forschungen und Fortschritte* 28 (1954), pp. 213–17. See also Aland's article, 'Die religiöse Haltung Kaiser Konstantins', in *Studia Patristica* (ed. Aland and Cross), I = Texte und Untersuchungen 63 (Berlin, 1957) pp. 549–600, reprinted in his collected papers, *Kirchengeschichtliche Entwürfe* (Gütersloh, 1960), pp. 202–39.

believe that a later forger would have troubled to search out the originals of old documents and copy them *in extenso*.'[1]

If Baynes' positive view of the documents in the *Vita Constantini* has been vindicated by the identification of the London papyrus, there is one substantial point of fact where new papyrus evidence has corrected him. On p. 16 (and note 54 on p. 82) Baynes tenaciously held to 323 as the date of Constantine's final victory over Licinius and attainment of sole mastery of the empire. His position was directed against Seeck, Jouguet, and especially E. Stein who, following the only ancient source to offer a date for this war,[2] placed Constantine's elimination of Licinius in 324. Baynes marshalled his arguments against Stein in the *Journal of Roman Studies* 18 (1929), pp. 218–19, the main consideration being the impossibility of squeezing in so much church history between September 324 and the council of Nicaea. Here, however, fresh evidence has proved Stein right and Baynes wrong.[3] An Oslo papyrus (P. Osl. ii, 44) contains two receipts: one is dated on the 6 Thoth (= 3 September) 'of the 19th and 17th and 9th year, 12th Indiction', the other on 30 Epiphi (= 24 July) 'of the 19th and 9th and 1st year, 13th Indiction'. These figures must mean (*a*) the 19th year of Constantine, 17th year of Licinius, 9th year of the Caesars Crispus, Constantine II, and Licinius junior, i.e. the year beginning (in the Egyptian calendar) on 29 August 324; and (*b*) the 19th year of Constantine, the 9th of the Caesars Crispus and Constantine (II), and the 1st of the Caesar Constantius (II) nominated Caesar on 8 November 324. The first receipt therefore belongs to 3 September 324, and presupposes that Licinius is still emperor at the time.

Baynes would no doubt have enlarged a reissue of his

[1] *Journal of Eccl. Hist.* 5 (1954), p. 200.

[2] *Consularia Constantinopolitana* ad ann. 324 (Mommsen, *Chronica Minora* i, p. 232).

[3] E. Stein, 'Konstantin d. Gr. gelangte 324 zur Alleinherrschaft', *Zeitschrift für die neutestamentliche Wissenschaft* 30 (1931), pp. 177–85. Baynes naturally conceded at once before this new evidence. See *Camb. Anc. Hist.* XII, p. 695.

lecture by a fresh survey of the main literature since 1930. Here it must suffice simply to catalogue the names of the authors of some of the principal studies and biographies: A. Piganiol (1932), E. Schwartz (revised edition, 1936), H. Berkhof (*Kirche und Kaiser*, 1947), A. H. M. Jones (1948), A. Alföldi (1948), J. Vogt (1949, revised edition 1960), P. Franchi de'Cavalieri (1953), H. Kraft (1955), L. Voelkl (1957), H. Dörries (1954 and 1958), S. Calderone (1962), R. MacMullen (1969), and J. Holland Smith (1971). There is also much relevant material in J. Straub, *Vom Herrscherideal in der Spätantike* (1939, reprinted 1964), and in his article 'Constantine as κοινὸς ἐπίσκοπος', *Dumbarton Oaks Papers* 21 (1967). E. Schwartz' papers on Athanasius, much admired by Baynes (p. 50), are in his *Gesammelte Schriften* 3 (1959).

HENRY CHADWICK

Christ Church, Oxford

RALEIGH LECTURE ON HISTORY

CONSTANTINE THE GREAT AND THE CHRISTIAN CHURCH

By NORMAN H. BAYNES

Read March 12, 1930

I MAKE no apology for the subject which I have chosen for my lecture—*Constantine the Great and the Christian Church*, for Constantine marks in his own person a turning-point in European history. No student of the Middle Ages can evade Constantine: he is one of the few inescapable figures in European history and one of the most intractable. To take man's past and demonstrate its inherent logic is a fascinating pursuit—to prove to one's own satisfaction that the past could not have been otherwise than it was, being a necessary development from that which had gone before, this is gratifying to man, for he can thus look back upon human history and regard it as in a sense his own creation and can then praise its creator. In this reconstruction of the past, however, difficulties are at times caused by the inter-position in the stream of history of outstanding personalities which resist rationalization and remain unexpected and embarrassing. One of these personalities is Constantine the Great. To my mind, at least, all attempts to explain away Constantine as the natural outcome of the previous history of Rome have failed completely.[1] Constantine can only be satisfactorily interpreted in terms of the Zeitgeist if the Zeit-geist is arbitrarily fashioned in the likeness of Constantine. The more closely Constantine's life and achievement are studied, the more inevitably is one driven to see in them an erratic block which has diverted the stream of human history. It may be true that by A.D. 311 the imperial policy of persecution of the Christians had been proved a failure —Galerius, the instigator of that policy, had publicly con-fessed its futility—but this failure could not carry with it the implication that it was the duty of a Roman Emperor so far to disavow Rome's past as himself to adopt the faith professed by perhaps one-tenth of his subjects.[2] Constantine presents to the student of history so interesting a problem precisely because he is an intractable individual, because he was not merely the creation of the past, but marked in himself a new beginning which was in such large measure to determine the future of the Roman world.

The representations attempted by modern scholars of the convictions and aims of Constantine have been so diverse that at times it is hard to believe that it is one and the same emperor that they are seeking to portray. As students of history we protest energetically that a man can only be rightly understood if he be regarded against the background of his world, that he can only be fairly judged in the light of the standards and the values of the society in which he lived; and then, having formulated the principle, we straightway forget it. We write our biographies in terms of the thought of our own day and impose upon another age the standards with which we are familiar.[3] Burckhardt began his famous chapter upon Constantine and the Christian Church with the remark:[4] 'In the case of a man of genius, whose ambition and love of power refuse to him a moment's peace, there can be no question of Christianity or paganism, of conscious religion or irreligion. Such a man even when he persuades himself that he has his place in an ecclesiastical community is essentially *un*religious.' The issue is thus, you observe, pre-judged, and the answer to the problem cannot be for an instant in doubt. Eusebius wrote a work which, had he been publishing it to-day, he would probably have entitled, 'Constantine and the Christian religion: a contribution towards imperial biography'.[5] After Burckhardt's opening sentence we may be sure that Eusebius will receive short shrift, and we are not disappointed. For the rationalist of the mid-nineteenth century there can be no hesitation: Constantine's supreme misfortune has been that the unhappy emperor fell into the hands of the most repulsive of all panegyrists who has falsified the portrait 'durch und durch'.[6] 'Eusebius is the first historian of antiquity who was *durch und durch* dishonest.'[7] But we may well ask: was any Roman of the fourth century 'essentially *un*religious'? 'In this age there were no such persons as free-thinkers', says M. Lot,[8] and he is probably not far from the truth.

Or again, consider Otto Seeck as he discusses the authenticity of documents attributed by Eusebius to Constantine: the belief that the divine will had punished those emperors who had persecuted the Christians and preserved those who had not enforced the edicts of persecution is, he notes, common to Lactantius, Eusebius, and the documents purporting to represent the thought of Constantine; the idea was in many men's minds. 'Why then should we be surprised if the good Constantine in his turn repeats the same trivialities?'[9] Trivialities? But what if a man really believes that God does actively, consistently, intervene in human affairs, that victory and defeat, prosperity and adversity are alike in His gift?—and what if that man is the ruler of the Roman world? Is that belief then insignificant? is it not rather of supreme moment? So hard it is to think ourselves back into a world which is not our own!

And there remains a yet subtler danger: we may imagine that we have discovered the key to a personality, and then we persuade ourselves that it will open every lock. And yet it is surely but rarely that every secret door of thought and motive in human life will yield to a single master-key. Life is not so simple as that. Eduard Schwartz has done as much as any scholar in our day to advance the study of the reign of Constantine; in his book, *The Emperor Constantine and the Christian Church*,[10] he has found the Open Sesame to the understanding of the reign in Constantine's resolution to exploit in his own interest the organization which gave to the Christian Church its corporate strength: through alliance with the Church Constantine sought to attain victory and the sole mastery of the Roman world.[11] The emperor's toleration sprang from his desire that pagan and Christian alike should be conscious that they depended upon him alone.[12] 'Never', writes Schwartz, 'has an emperor so triumphed over the Church as did Constantine in and through the Council of Nicaea';[13] the victory lay with the emperor's 'diabolical cleverness'.[14] The one man who opposed Constantine was Athanasius, and in that contest of wills Greek met Greek; for the opposition of Athanasius was inspired not by zeal for the true faith, not by any passion for the independence of the Church, but by the pride of a hierarch in the authority of his patriarchate.[15] The master-key in this analysis which Schwartz has given us of the personalities of Constantine and Athanasius is thus 'Der Wille zur Macht'. But it may be doubted whether so extreme a simplification can do justice to the complexity of human convictions and human motives. The solution would appear rather to be imposed upon the evidence than to arise from a patient study of the documents themselves.[16]

For myself, I have gradually come to the conviction that the true starting-point for any comprehension of the reign must be Constantine's own letters and edicts. That conclusion seems obvious enough, but so far as I am aware no one has yet consistently attempted from the evidence of these documents to sketch the aims and the thought of Constantine.[17] Indeed the student is met by the initial difficulty of determining which of these documents are genuine and which are simply forgeries, whether contemporary forgeries of Eusebius, of Athanasius, of Christians in the imperial chancery, or later forgeries from the reign of Constantius, from the time of Valentinian, or even from the hand of fifth-century interpolators.[18] My own view, which naturally you will not expect me to justify here, is that all the documents ascribed to Constantine in our sources are genuine, save only for a doubt in respect of the sermon addressed *To the Assembly of the Saints*. In the Greek version of that sermon, which alone has been preserved to us, I find it difficult to believe that we have a faithful translation of the Latin original as delivered by Constantine.[19] I have therefore excluded it from our consideration this afternoon. So far as is possible, I have tried to avoid prepossessions; I desire that these documents may speak for themselves; from them let us try to outline the relations of Constantine towards the Christian Church.

A few words will suffice to rough in the background. In A.D. 293 Diocletian made Constantine's father, Constantius Chlorus, Caesar; he became the colleague of the western Augustus, Maximianus Herculius, the earthly representative of the divine Hercules.[20] It was Constantius Chlorus who brought back Britain to the Roman allegiance after the overthrow of Carausius. Constantine himself did not remain with his father in the West, but lived at the court of Diocletian in Nicomedia or served his apprenticeship in arms under the Caesar Galerius. He was thus present in the East when in 303 Galerius forced upon Diocletian the policy of persecution.[21] In 305 Diocletian left to Galerius the task of carrying on the bloody repression of Christianity which the Caesar had initiated, and together with Diocletian the western Augustus, Maximian, also abdicated.[22] In the West, Constantius Chlorus became Augustus with Galerius for his eastern colleague. Constantine, summoned to Britain by his father, was acclaimed emperor by the army on the death of Constantius: he becomes a sovereign of the Herculian dynasty. The deities to whom he owes special devotion are thus Jupiter, the divine protector of the Jovian dynasty founded by Diocletian, and Hercules.[23] When Maximian had reassumed the purple, becoming for a second time Augustus, and had given his daughter Fausta in marriage to Constantine, the association with the Herculian dynasty was rendered yet more intimate. But Maximian, seeking to remove Constantine, met his death; the Herculian line was discredited, and Constantine sought a new title for his sovereignty. He discovered that he was descended from Claudius II, the emperor who in the third century had stayed the Gothic invasion of the empire.[24] The new title to rule carried with it a religious conversion: Constantine acknowledges as his divine protector the god whom his own family had worshipped—the Sun. In an age of religious syncretism this cult of the Sun adopted by the ruler of the Gallic provinces derives from many sources. Behind it lies the sun-worship of the Danubian provinces whence Constantine's family had migrated to the West; behind it lies the sun-worship of Zoroastrian Persia, and Aurelian's cult of the Unconquered Sun brought back from his eastern campaigns; while it was readily associated with the wide-spread Gallic worship of Apollo as god of light and healing and of sacred spring. And since this worship had been ancestral in Constantine's house, the Sun stands as symbol of the dynasty, the Claudian dynasty of the Second Flavians.[25] Constantius had refused in the West to execute the bloody edicts; under Constantine the West continued to enjoy religious peace. In 311 Galerius abandoned the policy of persecution: he capitulated, published his edict of toleration, and implored the prayers of the persecuted.[26] That appeal was of no avail: a fortnight later he was dead, and Licinius was emperor in his room. In the West, Maxentius the son of Maximian held Italy, and on his father's death broke with Constantine and concluded an alliance with the eastern Caesar Maximin.[27] It was a moment of crisis for Constantine: his forces were outnumbered by those of Maxentius; the latter had collected huge supplies of corn from Africa, and these were stored within the granaries of Rome; the newly-built walls of Aurelian made the western capital impregnable; two armies which had previously marched into Italy against Maxentius had perished miserably. In Rome Maxentius was supported by pagan prophets and augurs who promised victory, and in an age when it was really believed that victory or defeat was in the gift of Heaven, the sure promise of victory meant much: it was indeed by no means the 'triviality' which it may appear to a modern rationalist. It will be sufficient to remind you of the Battle of the Frigidus (A.D. 395).[28]   The gods of Rome, then, had declared for Maxentius; whence in this crisis should Constantine seek aid?   Years later the emperor affirmed to Eusebius that he had seen a vision of the cross athwart the sun, and, beneath, the words, 'In this conquer'.[29]   Where Constantine was at this time, Eusebius does not tell us; a late legendary account says at Arles.[30]   That account has in itself no historical value, but it is at least *ben trovato*. That is all the historian can say: 'Eusebius asserts that Constantine affirmed to him' . . . but yet it is not quite all; he can add that against the advice of his generals, against the counsel of the augurs, with amazing daring Constantine invaded Italy, and having defeated in the north of the peninsula the troops of Maxentius, took the still more surprising step of marching directly against the fortifications of the western capital.   To my mind, I confess, this is more explicable if Constantine was convinced that the Christian God had assured him victory.   Whether that appearance of the cross of light was only a subjective experience or whether it was an objective reality[31] the historian cannot decide.   Still less can he determine whether it was a God-granted miracle; to answer such a question the historian must turn philosopher or theologian; as historian he is perforce silent.   He is unable to affirm miracle, but most certainly he cannot deny it.   Just as is the case with Paul on the road to Damascus, so with Constantine in his hour of crisis the historian can but discuss the value of his sources and state the result of his criticism.   Eusebius asserts that Constantine affirmed . . .   For our purpose we may leave it at that: each of us according to his view of the world can then proceed either with Franchi de' Cavalieri, with Şesan and Knöpfler to assert miracle, or with Schrörs and Seeck and Burckhardt to deny the direct intervention of God.[32]

And before the walls of Rome a vision came to Constantine bidding him place upon the shields of his soldiers the Christian monogram.[33]   That command was obeyed, and the Sybilline books foretelling the defeat of the enemy of Rome drove Maxentius from the shelter of the walls of Aurelian to disaster and to death on the banks of the Tiber.[34] The God of the Christians had kept His word. Constantine, as the inscription of the triumphal arch testifies,[35] had saved the Roman state from the tyrant and his faction *instinctu divinitatis, mentis magnitudine.* There may be ambiguity in those words, but I would still translate them 'by the prompting of the divinity, by the emperor's own greatness of mind'; they are contrasted, not parallel phrases.[36]

Constantine, hailed as senior Augustus by the senate, forthwith used his authority to dispatch to Maximin an order to stay the persecution and to issue a new decree of toleration.[37] It is probable that at the same time—still in A.D. 312—he wrote to Anullinus,[38] pro-consul in Africa, ordering him to restore to the churches all property which had formerly belonged to the Catholic Church in whosesoever hands that property—'gardens, houses or anything else'—might now be; while he informed Caecilianus,[39] the Catholic bishop of Carthage, that instructions had been sent to the imperial *rationalis* in Africa to provide funds for distribution amongst the Catholics of Africa, Numidia, and Mauretania. Constantine, I would suggest, wrote these letters from Rome; already he knows of the Donatist schism in Africa and condemns it as a vain and bastard delusion (φαύλη ὑπονόθευσις). A little later, but before April 313, he gives orders to Anullinus that the Catholic clergy shall be freed from all public liturgies (*munera civilia*). The interest of this letter lies in the reason given for the granting of this privilege[40]—remember that Constantine is writing not to a Christian bishop, but to an imperial governor. 'Since it appears from many considerations that through the setting at nought of the ritual (θρησκεία) in which the chief reverence for the most holy heavenly (power) is preserved great dangers have been brought upon the state, but when that ritual has been regularly resumed and is observed, there has resulted the greatest good fortune to the Roman name and remarkable prosperity in all human affairs, the divine beneficence granting this', therefore those who devote their lives to this service should have their reward. Already in Constantine's thought the Catholic priests through their priesthood are maintaining the fortunes of Rome. This is more than mere tolerance.

In February 313 Licinius met Constantine at Milan, and there married Constantine's sister.[41] At this meeting a policy of complete religious freedom was agreed upon; the corporation of the Christian Church—or rather, perhaps, of each separate Christian Church—was recognized as a legal person; the text was doubtless settled of a rescript which would be put into force by Licinius on his return to the East. It is that text which is generally known as the Edict of Milan. Seeck has shown that we cannot prove that there ever was an Edict published at Milan; it is indeed unlikely that any such edict was issued, but this is so because in all probability Constantine had anticipated the agreement in policy reached at Milan in rescripts similar to that directed to Anullinus, which had been sent to all the governors of the Western provinces. The Edict of Milan may be a fiction, but the fact for which the term stood remains untouched.[42] Licinius left Milan to carry to the Christians of the East the message of toleration, recognition, and restitution framed by the senior Augustus. He was met by the revolt of his Caesar Maximin; after Maximin's defeat and death the mastery of the Roman world was shared between Licinius and Constantine.

Only a few months had passed since the victory of the Milvian Bridge when Constantine's exclusion of the Donatists from the imperial benefactions was challenged: the schismatics appealed to the emperor praying that he would appoint judges from Gaul to settle the dispute.[43] Constantine accepted the petition, chose three Gallic bishops, and wrote to the Pope and a certain Marcus[44] directing them, together with their Gallic colleagues, to examine the ten

Donatist and ten Catholic representatives from Africa and thus determine the issue. It is, says Constantine, very grievous to him that a large number of his subjects in lands which the divine providence has entrusted to him should be found persistently turning to vanity (ἐπὶ τὸ φαυλότερον) and that bishops should be at variance with one another. The Pope and Marcus are to rest assured that Constantine pays such reverence to the lawfully constituted Catholic Church that he desires that they should nowhere leave in any place schism or discord. The emperor, you will observe, has set up an ecclesiastical tribunal of five judges; the Pope, following the practice of the Church, transforms this tribunal into a council by adding fourteen Italian bishops.[45] This is important, for in the following year Constantine shows by summoning the Council of Arles that he has learnt his lesson.

The Pope gave his judgement in favour of Caecilian, the Catholic bishop of Carthage, but against that decision the Donatists protested. Constantine determined that the dispute, which should have spontaneously (αὐθαιρέτῳ συγκαθέσει) settled itself after the Roman judgement, should be finally concluded by a more representative tribunal (πολλῶν παρόντων). The letter which the emperor wrote to his vicar in Africa when making arrangements for the new council is interesting.[46] Constantine desires a settlement of the controversy 'because it gives an opportunity for criticism to those who are known to turn their minds away from this most holy religion'. Constantine is already concerned for the mission of the Church to the pagan world. At the close of the letter the emperor thus addresses Aelafius:

'I consider it by no means right that contentions and altercations of this kind should be hidden from me, by which, perchance, God may be moved not only against the human race, but also against me myself, to whose care by His heavenly decree He has entrusted the direction of all human affairs, and may in His wrath provide otherwise than heretofore. For then shall I be able to remain truly and most fully without anxiety, and may always hope for all most prosperous and excellent things from the ever-ready kindness

of the most powerful God when I shall know that all, bound together in brotherly concord, adore the most holy God with the
worship of the Catholic religion which is His due.'

'God may be moved against me myself'—to secure the unity
of the Church falls within the charge committed to a
Roman emperor.

The Council of Arles reaffirmed the judgement of Rome:
once more the Donatists protested and petitioned the
emperor personally to judge the issue. The letter which
the emperor sent to the bishops assembled at Arles before
they returned to their sees is of great significance for the
biography of Constantine; the whole letter deserves careful
study. I can quote only a few extracts:

> 'The incomprehensible kindness of our God'—note the pronoun[47]
> —'by no means allows the state of man to stray for too long a time
> in the darkness, nor does it suffer the odious wills of some so to
> prevail as not to grant men a new opportunity for conversion to
> the truth (*iustitiam*) by opening up before them through its most
> glorious light a path to salvation. Of this indeed I am assured by
> many examples and I can illustrate the same truth from my own
> case. For at the first there were in me things which appeared far
> removed from the truth (*iustitia carere*) and I did not think that
> there was any heavenly power which could see into the secrets of
> my heart. What fortune ought these things which I have men-
> tioned to have brought upon me?—surely one overflowing with
> every evil. But Almighty God, Who sitteth in the watch-tower of
> Heaven, has bestowed upon me that which I did not deserve. Truly,
> most holy bishops of the Saviour Christ, at this time I can neither
> describe nor number these gifts which of His heavenly benevolence
> He has granted to me, his servant (*famulum suum*).'

The emperor congratulates the bishops on their decision
which should recall to the truth those whom the malignity
of the devil seemed to have alienated from the glorious light
of the Catholic law (*legis catholicae*), who in their war against
the truth had joined themselves to the gentiles (*gentibus*):

> 'But that judgement has been of no avail since so great a mad-
> ness holds the Donatists captive that with unbelievable arrogance
> they persuade themselves of things which may not be said or heard,
> departing from the right judgement which has been given, from

which, as by Heaven's provision I have learnt, they are appealing to my judgement. Oh! what force has the wickedness which still persists in their breasts. . . . They ask judgement from me who am myself awaiting the judgement of Christ; for I declare, as is the truth, that the judgement of bishops ought to be looked upon as if the Lord Himself were sitting in judgement. . . . They have instituted an appeal as is done in the lawsuits of the pagans; for pagans are accustomed at times to avoid the lower courts where justice can be quickly discerned and through the intervention of the authorities to resort to an appeal to the higher courts. What is to be said of these defamers of the law who rejecting the judgement of Heaven have thought that they should demand judgement from me? Do they thus think of Christ the Saviour? They are self-confessed betrayers. . . . Do you return to your own sees. As for these wicked deceivers of religion I have given instructions to my men to bring them to my court that there they may stay and may behold something worse than death. And I have sent letters to the vicarius of Africa with orders that as often as he finds any sharing in this madness he should send them at once to my court, lest under so great a shining of our God they should be guilty of spreading further that which may arouse the greatest wrath of the Providence of Heaven.'

You will notice the recurrence of this thought. That fear does, I feel, form a vital element in Constantine's religious policy.

In the autumn of 314 came the first war with Licinius, and the emperor was detained in the Danube lands until the summer of 315. On 21 July 315 he re-entered Rome. On his arrival the Donatist bishops asked for permission to return to Africa; Constantine had consented and had chosen friends of his to try the issue in Africa and there end the dispute. A few days later, however, he changed his mind. He feared that Donatist violence might prevent a satisfactory trial; through their obstinacy the issue might be displeasing to the celestial divinity and damaging to his own reputation (*quam semper inlibatam cupio perseverare*), an interesting conjunction. The emperor summons Caecilian to the court and promises the Donatists: 'If you are able to prove one charge or crime against him in his presence, then for me the position will be the same as if you had

proved all your accusations'. For some undisclosed reason
—perhaps simply that the time allowed was too short—
Caecilian did not reach Rome before Constantine left the
city for Milan, where we find him on 19 October. At Milan
after Caecilian's arrival the emperor was prepared to try
the case, had not the Donatist accusers attempted to escape
from the city. Philumenus[48] then suggested a new plan:
let Caecilian and Donatus both be retained in Italy while
an episcopal commission was sent to Africa to appoint a
new bishop of Carthage.[49] Constantine accepted the suggestion; the request of Donatus to return to Carthage was refused,[50] while Caecilian was kept at Brescia. Two bishops
left for Africa. But the project came to nought; Donatus
escaped and Caecilian followed him to Carthage. When
the news reached Constantine at Trier early in 316, he
realized that he would after all be forced personally to
intervene. The Donatist bishops were provided with a
passport and instructions were sent to the vicar of Africa
to leave the schismatics for a time in peace. Constantine
announced that he would himself shortly come to Africa
where he would read a judgement free from all ambiguity
which would set forth the whole course of the dispute and
would demonstrate what and what kind of veneration
should be shown towards the supreme divinity, and what
sort of worship would appear to be pleasing to Him.
Those who do not worship the supreme God with fitting
veneration 'perdam atque discutiam'—'I will destroy and
disperse'. The letter closes with the words: 'I believe that
by no means can I in any way escape the greatest guilt save
by bringing wickedness to light. What can be done by me
more consonant with my fixed resolve and with the duty
of an emperor than, having dissipated errors and cut off all
unfounded opinions, to cause all men to present to omni-
potent God true religion, unfeigned concord, and the worship which is His due.' But Constantine knew well the
difficulty of such a course; the Donatists would pose as
martyrs, and though he protested that it was obvious that

no one could obtain the beatitudes of a martyr through suffering for irreligion and violence—that would be alien from the truth of religion and incongruous—he yet hesitated to take the final step. In the end he did not go to Africa, but in November 316[51] he gave his judgement in favour of Caecilian which set forth how it came to be that *post episcopalia iudicia* the emperor had determined the issue.[52] At the same time by an imperial constitution the Donatist churches were confiscated and handed over to the imperial treasury. The military repression of Donatism began, the Donatist calendar of martyrs was formed. Four years later Constantine was forced to admit defeat, the Donatist exiles were recalled, and by an *ignominiosissima indulgentia*—the phrase is Augustine's—the schismatics were left to the judgement of God.

The story is not usually told at this length in our textbooks, and yet to my mind it is the essential prelude to the understanding of Constantine's conduct after his conquest of the East from Licinius. The eastern Augustus had felt that his Christian subjects looked with envious eyes upon the men of the West governed by an emperor who made no secret of his devotion to the Christian God; gradually Licinius drifted into a petty persecution of the Christians; the martyrs were few, and those did not perish by the orders of Licinius, but through the officious zeal of his agents. Yet once more the Civil Service[53] was purified of Christians, and Christians were forced to participate in pagan ceremonies. The war between the two Augusti, fought in A.D. 323,[54] is represented as a religious war in the history of Eusebius, and I see no reason to doubt that such was its character in the eyes of Constantine. The defeat of Licinius was straightway followed by the issue of two edicts preserved in a Greek version by Eusebius in his panegyric on Constantine. The authenticity of these texts is still denied by many scholars, though I think without good reason. We have seen that immediately after the Battle of the Milvian Bridge Constantine had granted privileges to the Christians, so now after the battle of Chrysopolis the emperor declares that his policy remains unchanged. In the former of the two edicts Constantine first deals with the restoration to the Christians of personal rights and then of rights to property. The edict is the great measure of 'liquidation' terminating the whole period of the persecutions from A.D. 303 onward.[55] Constantine knew in what way Maximin had interpreted the edict of toleration issued by Galerius: had Licinius secured a faithful application of the religious policy which had been agreed upon at Milan? In any event doubts should be ended, and a comprehensive measure should inaugurate the new régime. We may presume that Constantine was familiar with the work of Lactantius—he had summoned the Christian rhetorician from the East to Gaul to be the tutor of his son—and the argument of the *De Mortibus Persecutorum* had just been signally vindicated: Licinius proclaiming the policy concerted at Milan had overthrown the persecutor Maximin, Licinius turned persecutor had been dethroned by Constantine. The edict begins with a lengthy exposition of the theme of Lactantius' pamphlet. 'Trivialities', says Seeck, but whether you believe this philosophy of human history or not, you must surely confess that the vision of Jewish prophet and Christian apologist of a God living in and through human history is a majestic conception; you will admit that, should a ruler happen to believe it, it must have for him a greater practical significance than any other consideration. For the evils of the age of persecution God had found the remedy in Constantine:

'God sought my service and judged that service fitted to achieve His purpose. Starting from Britain God had scattered the evil powers that mankind might be recalled to true religion instructed through my agency, and that the blessed faith might spread under His guiding hand. And from the West, believing that this gift had been entrusted to myself, I have come to the East which was in sorer need of my aid. At the same time I am absolutely persuaded that I owe my whole life, my every breath, and in a word my most secret thoughts to the supreme God.'

Do you not catch the echo? Constantine had once imagined that no divine power could penetrate to the secrets of his heart. It would be strange, Constantine proceeds, if the glory of the confessors should not be raised to greater splendour and blessedness under the rule of the servant of God. We remember again the phrase 'the *famulus* of God' from the earlier letter: θεράπων here probably represents the same Latin original.

The second of the two edicts preserved by Eusebius is a confession of faith. It begins with a repetition of the argument derived from the melancholy deaths of the persecutors: the violence of the polytheist ending in destruction, the mercy and the piety of Constantine's father the monotheist, the worshipper of the Saviour God, transmitting his rule to his son.[56] Constantine's sense of his mission is reasserted; he prays God to grant to the much tried eastern provinces healing through His servant:

'Not unreasonably do I make this prayer to Thee, Lord of the universe, Holy God. Under Thy leading have I attempted and accomplished deeds which have brought salvation (σωτηριώδη πράγματα); everywhere with Thy seal as my protection (i.e. the sign of the cross on the Christian standard, the labarum) I have led my army to victory, and, if the need of the state should summon me, following the same symbols of Thy virtue, I will go forth against the foe.'

But the real interest of the edict lies in Constantine's declaration of policy towards the pagans. His desire is that his people should remain in peace and concord for the common advantage of the inhabited world and of all men. 'Let those who are in error be free to enjoy the same peace and quietude as those who believe. Let no one molest another; let each hold to that which his soul desires and let him use this to the full. But as for the wise—it is right that they should be persuaded that those alone will live a holy and pure life whom Thou, O God, callest to find rest in Thy holy laws.' Later he repeats the same counsel adding, 'For it is one thing to enter voluntarily upon the

struggle for immortality, another to compel others to do
so from fear of punishment'. He has explained his position
at length, 'since some think, as I hear, that the rites of the
temples and the power of darkness have been abolished.
That indeed I would have recommended to all men if it
had not been that the violent revolt of wicked error were not
immoderately fixed in the minds of some to the injury of
the common salvation.' There is, it should freely be admitted, no precise parallel elsewhere in Constantine's writings to this expression of policy, but the same spirit of
scornful tolerance breathes through not a few of his edicts.
As the years passed toleration of paganism gave place to
active repression; the emperor felt that he was strong enough
to advance to a frontal attack upon paganism. The important fact to realize, however, is that this alteration in policy
entailed no change of spirit, only a change of method. What
Constantine would have recommended in 323 he later
felt free to proclaim as the imperial will.[57] The emperor,
addressing the world of his new pagan subjects in the
eastern provinces, allays their fears by announcing toleration for the old believers; those who deny the authenticity
of the edict have no easy task before them when they seek
a plausible motive for the falsification of the document.[58]

Constantine had come to the East with high hopes; he
found the Eastern Church rent by the Arian controversy.
Would there be in the Christian East another Donatist
schism? He sent his trusted counsellor Hosius of Cordova
to Alexandria with a letter addressed to the bishop Alexander and the presbyter Arius.[59] This is a very remarkable
document. In it Constantine first states his aims in marching to the East: one was to heal the body of the Roman
world which was suffering from a severe wound; that aim
was achieved by military force in the overthrow of Licinius;
the other was to unite his subjects in one common religious
belief. 'I knew that, if in accordance with my prayers I could
establish a common agreement amongst all the servants of
God, then the need of the state would as the fruit of that

agreement undergo a change in consonance with the pious
desires of all.' The only way in which it seemed to the
emperor possible to cure the Donatist disorders was that
envoys from the Eastern Church should be sent to Africa
on a mission of conciliation. Christianity had arisen in the
East and thence spread through the world; the Easterners
were therefore the natural missionaries for the world's
salvation. 'No sooner was the victory achieved than my
first inquiry was directed to this end which I thought to
be of greater value and moment than anything else.' The
bitter disappointment of the failure in Africa had left its
mark upon the soul of Constantine.

And now, in place of union, battles of words about abstruse
points which might perhaps have provided an exercise for
philosophic debate, but should rather be kept imprisoned
in the mind, not rashly made public nor thoughtlessly disclosed to the ears of the multitude. Let Alexander and
Arius take a lesson from the philosophers who if they dis-
agree on *one* point still act in concert to maintain the unity
of philosophic doctrine. How much more should we who
are constituted servants of the great God be of one mind
in the fundamental beliefs of our religion! Constantine
offers himself as a mediator of peace in this dispute:[60] he
pleads that he, the servant of God—a phrase now familiar
to us—may be allowed under Providence to bring God's
people by his words and help and counsel to a renewed
communion. The emperor had hoped to visit the provinces
won from Licinius, but was restrained from so doing that
he might not be compelled to see with his own eyes things
which even to hear of he had thought an impossibility.
'Open to me by your unity the road to the East!' For our
purpose the letter is of interest as evidence of Constantine's
conviction that he was called to play the part of providential
mediator between the disputants.

The mission of Hosius failed; bishops assembled at
Antioch condemned Arius and fixed on Ancyra as the town
in which a larger council should assemble to formulate with

greater authority the standpoint of the Eastern Church. Ancyra was the see of Marcellus, the champion of the extreme view diametrically opposed to that of Arius. The emperor, who had expressed the desire to act as mediator, should be faced with a *fait accompli*.[61] It was shrewd tactics, but Constantine, who naturally did not desire the victory of either extreme, was equal to the occasion. He commandeered the Council of Ancyra by proposing to make it not merely representative of the Eastern Church, but oecumenical in its range. Then, having possessed himself of the initiative, he transferred the council to Nicaea where its deliberations would be subject to his own control. At that council, I believe, Constantine acted as President and as such directed its proceedings towards the adoption of his own solution—the Homoousion. Whence Constantine derived that solution we need not ask here: it may well have come not from Hosius, but from some eastern adviser of the emperor. The important point to notice is that Constantine, who while in the West had written 'lecto dilucido iudicio demonstraturus sum quae et qualis divinitati adhibenda veneratio', was now given his great opportunity.[62] He had his answer ready, and to that answer he remained loyal throughout his reign. The solution was so successful that the council found it necessary to excommunicate only two bishops.[63]

The letters written after Nicaea are filled with Constantine's gratitude for the success of his efforts to secure unity. 'From the divine Providence we have received fulness of grace that we may, freed from all error, acknowledge one and the same faith. No longer can the devil work his will against us', his plots have been overthrown by the bishops, and in that triumph Constantine could claim no small share. 'That this end might be attained, by the will of God I summoned to the city of Nicaea as many bishops as possible with whom I, your fellow-servant, as one of your number rejoiced above measure to be present and myself received the exposition of the truth.' To those bishops who were

not at the council he wrote: 'Having learned from the prosperity of the state how great is the favour of the divine power, I considered that before everything else my aim should be that among the most blessed congregations of the Catholic Church there should be observed one faith, love unalloyed, and piety towards God, the Lord of all, unsullied by discord.'[64] The way was now open for the emperor's projected visit to the eastern provinces—the way which the Arian controversy had closed.

But still the priest who had initiated that controversy, Arius, remained outside the Church; it was not long before he too surrendered to the imperial servant of God.[65] We still possess Constantine's letter of triumph reporting that success to Alexander, the bishop of Alexandria:

'Arius, *the* Arius, I tell you, has come to me, the Augustus, with the assurance that he holds the same views concerning the Catholic faith as those defined by you at the Council of Nicaea. . . . I have talked with him in the presence of many others concerning the word of life. I, as you know well (ἐγώ εἰμι ὁ ἄνθρωπος ἐκεῖνος), with unalloyed faith have devoted my mind to God; I am your fellow-servant whose constant care has been the establishment of concord . . . I implore you to receive those who come as suppliants. Haste, I beseech you, to the help of concord. Let me hear from you what I wish and desire—the peace and unity of you all.'

At the resumed session of the Council of Nicaea two years after its first meeting the excommunicated bishops could be welcomed back to the Church and the conversion of Arius announced.[66] But neither Alexander nor his successor Athanasius was prepared to rejoice over the sinner who had repented.[67] To Athanasius Constantine wrote: 'Now you know my will: to all those who desire to enter the Church do you provide free entry. For if I hear that you have hindered any who share in the faith of the Church or that you have barred such from entering in, I will immediately send one who at my order shall depose you and shall drive you into exile.' Still Athanasius remained impenitent. At length Arius grew weary of this delay in his recognition: he threatened to secede from orthodoxy. The letter which

Constantine addressed to him and his supporters is an astonishing document; it is so improbable that for that very reason it is impossible to regard it as a forgery. The armoury of abuse is ransacked: Constantine here turns theologian and defends the single οὐσία—the one essence—of Father and of Son. As God's man (ὁ σὸς ἄνθρωπος) he appeals to God to support his words so far as they are true. The Erythraean Sibyl more than three thousand years before had prophesied the madness of Arius. 'You, Arius, have done your best with your blasphemies to throw into confusion the whole inhabited world. Don't you see that I, the man of God, already understand all your devices? Your whole scheme is vain; in a moment the fires which you have kindled will be extinguished by the rains of God.' But through this storm of invective the emperor still remembers his vision of unity. 'Look you, once more I come as a suppliant. I could fight: I could overwhelm with arms the body of your supporters, however large it be. But such is not my will. Guarded by the faith of Christ I wish to heal you and yours.' The letter closes with a dramatic appeal: 'You, you man with a mind of iron, come to me, come, I say, to the man of God, and if you will surrender your madness and call upon the divine grace, I will heal you. If you recognize the light of truth, I will give thanks to God.' Constantine was ready, as was not Athanasius, to pardon the prodigal son.

Despite the emperor's threatening letter to Athanasius the messenger was not sent to deprive the bishop of his see; the personality of Athanasius clearly impressed Constantine, and on one occasion the emperor intervened in his favour. Athanasius made no response to the summons bidding him attend the Council of Caesarea. At length in 335 Constantine determined to bring to a decision the dispute between the Eusebian party and the patriarch of Alexandria. The bishops should meet at Tyre. 'It would perhaps be natural and peculiarly fitting considering the prosperity of the times', wrote the emperor, 'that the Catholic Church should be at unity within itself, and that those who are now the servants of Christ should be free from all recriminations.' You note the constantly recurring thought of the close connexion between the fortunes of the state and the unity of the Church. But since this is not so, Constantine directs the bishops to come at a run, as the saying goes, to heal the wounds of the Church:

'Unity, you will agree, is pleasing to the Lord God: if you could re-establish it, it would redound to your credit, it would for us all be more even than we have asked in our prayers. Therefore let there be no delay on your part. I have given directions that those bishops shall be present whom you desire to share your deliberations, and, if anyone—which I do not expect—should still ignore our summons, I will send one who at my command shall drive him forth and shall teach him that it is unseemly for him to resist an emperor's orders when issued in defence of the truth. It will be for you to judge without hatred or partiality.'

Athanasius hesitated long in pitiful uncertainty, as we know from the papyri published by Mr. Bell,[68] but ultimately he obeyed and travelled to Tyre. Before the hostility of the Eusebian party he fled to Constantinople, and appealed directly to the emperor. He was able to convince Constantine that he was the victim of the rancour of his foes. The bishops were summoned to the capital to explain their action. 'It must be the work of divine Providence,' writes the emperor, 'to show to us clearly whether you have indeed judged without partiality or hatred.' Before me— whom not even you would deny to be the true servant of God—you must establish the real course of events. I have found Athanasius so low, so humbled that you would have unbounded pity at the sight of him. He has asked to be faced with his accusers: it is a reasonable request. Therefore I bid you come with all speed and make your defence.

Arius had just been formally received back into communion with the Church at Jerusalem. At the interview which followed the arrival in Constantinople of the Eusebian leaders Athanasius enraged the emperor. It can hardly be doubted that he renewed his refusal to communicate with the heresiarch. For the moment Constantine's patience was exhausted and the bishop was banished to Gaul. But still no successor was appointed to the see of Alexandria; the emperor awaited the submission of Athanasius: that alone was needed to complete his triumph. When Constantine died in 337, Athanasius was still in exile.[69]

There remains only to be considered Constantine's role as 'bishop of those without the Church'[70] whether heretics or pagans; and, in particular, reference must be made to two letters, that addressed to the heretics, and the letter to the Persian King Sapor. The former opens with a rhetorical exordium in which Constantine confesses that he has not the leisure to describe the evils which are caused by the heretics. Under the pretence of godliness you befoul everything; pure and innocent consciences you wound by your death-dealing blows. The very daylight, one might almost say, you snatch from the eyes of men. This is the justification for the emperor's intervention. Why should we longer endure such ills? Our long-suffering causes even the healthy to be infected as with a plague. Why then do we not with all speed through punishments inflicted by the state cut out the evil by the roots? The emperor proceeds to order the confiscation of the churches of the heretics and to forbid any gathering for worship. Rather, instead of meeting in heretical conventicles let them come to the Catholic Church and share in its holiness: 'Thus you will be enabled to attain to the truth. For it becomes that blessedness, which our age enjoys under God's favour, that men who live with good hopes for their guide should be led from all their disordered wanderings into the straight path, from darkness to light, from vanity to truth, from death to salvation.' This is the same voice which had thundered against the Donatists. Had Constantine learnt nothing from his African failure? asks Monsignor Batiffol, who considers the letter to be a forgery.[71] He had left the Donatists to the judgement of God, but that admission of his own ill success could not alter the fact of an emperor's duty 'ut discussis erroribus . . . veram religionem atque meritam omnipotenti deo culturam praesentare perficiat'. We are told by Sozomen* that the law was not enforced against the large body of Montanists in Phrygia, while the Novatians who were orthodox in their belief were expressly protected by a constitution of A.D. 326. We shall never understand such expressions of the imperial will as this letter of Constantine unless we realize that they were intended as propaganda, in Sozomen's words, 'to terrify rather than to destroy the emperor's subjects'. The execution of such edicts would be left to the discretion of the local authorities. The heart of this letter lies in the appeal to the heretics to return to the Catholic Church; it is the natural result of the charge laid upon the emperor as ἐπίσκοπος τῶν ἔξω (τῆς ἐκκλησίας).

Lastly we come to the letter addressed to the Persian king. It begins with the emperor's confession of his Christian faith. It tells how, with the power of the Christian God as his ally, starting from the bounds of Ocean he had in successive stages raised the entire οἰκουμένη—the Roman world—upon the basis of firm hopes of salvation; the slavery of many tyrants had been banished and avenged. 'This God I serve, Whose sign my army, dedicated to God, bears on its shoulders; to whatever tasks the word of justice calls it that army marches, and straightway for these enterprises I receive His grace in manifest trophies of victory.' There follows an attack upon paganism which has destroyed whole peoples. God hates pride and overthrows it, while the faithful are granted His aid and live in peace. Those Roman emperors who persecuted Christianity have been swept away: Valerian, Sapor will remember, paid the penalty as a prisoner of Persia. 'I have myself seen the vengeance of God wrought upon the persecutors. I am convinced that the greatest safety and prosperity will be enjoyed everywhere when God through the pure and righteous worship of the Christians and from their agree-

* *H.E.* ii. 32.

ment concerning the divinity shall deign to draw all men unto Himself.' Constantine rejoices to hear that there is a large company of Christians within the Persian empire, and he wishes good fortune to the Persian king and to his Christian subjects: so he will find in the Lord of all a father, a God of grace and favour. Because the Persian king is known for his piety Constantine entrusts the Christians to his charge. 'Love them as befits your love of man. So through the faith there shall come to yourself and to us a blessing.'

A remarkable letter, an improbable letter: already the reader feels himself in the atmosphere of the Middle Ages. But is it an impossible letter? Nowhere else, it has been objected, does Constantine display this missionary enthusiasm. But is that true? In the early years of his reign he had deplored the Donatist schism because it prejudiced Christianity in the eyes of the pagans. In the speech with which the emperor opened the Council of Nicaea he is reported to have said: 'For truly it would be a terrible thing—a very terrible thing—that now when wars are ended and none dares to offer further resistance we should begin to attack each other and thus give cause for pleasure and for laughter to the pagan world (τοῖς δυσμενέσιν· cf. letter to Aelafius: 'quae . . . etiam his hominibus detrahendi dent facultatem qui longe ab huiuscemodi sanctissima observantia sensus suos noscuntur avertere).' With the crusade which brought Constantine from the furthest West to the Roman East we are already familiar, but that passage appears in the Edict to the Provincials (*V.C.* ii. 28), and the authenticity of that document is questioned. Constantine's letter, however, directed against Eusebius and Theognius is now unchallenged; here we read:

'You know me your fellow-servant, you know the pledge of your salvation which I have in all sincerity made my care and through which we have not only conquered the armed force of our foes, but have also enclosed their souls alive to demonstrate the true faith of the love of man. But at this success I rejoiced most of all

C

because it resulted in the renewal of the οἰκουμένη. And indeed it is a thing to wonder at that so many peoples should be brought to the same mind—peoples which but yesterday were said to be in ignorance of God. And think of what they might have learnt if no shadow of strife had come upon them! Why then, my be-loved brothers, tell me, why do I bring a charge against you? We are Christians, and yet we are torn by pitiable disagreements.'

The letter which Constantine wrote to the bishops who had condemned Athanasius at Tyre as reported by Athanasius is also now unquestioned; in that letter Constantine writes:

'Through my service toward God peace is established on every hand and even the greater number of barbarian peoples truly reverence the name of God—peoples which till now were ignorant of the truth—and clearly he who does not know the truth cannot recognize God. As I say, even the barbarians themselves now on account of me, the sincere servant of God, have recognized God and have learnt to reverence Him Who, as they realize from His very acts, protects me and everywhere cares for me. And of this the all-important consequence is that they know God and reverence Him on account of their fear of us. And we who appear as the champions of the holy mysteries of His grace . . . we give ourselves up to discord and hatred.'

What drew Constantine towards Athanasius was that he had a gift for winning over the pagans to Christianity.[72] These passages in uncontested letters of Constantine are surely in their thought precisely parallel to the argument of the letter to Sapor, and it must never be forgotten that when the Persian king betrayed his trust and attacked the Christian Armenians, it was to Constantine that the Armenians appealed, it was Constantine's intervention which restored the Christian kingdom of Armenia.[73] On these passages I would base my argument for the authenticity of the letter, but to them I would add another citation which I personally believe to be no forgery, viz.: Constantine's statement that Christians during the great persecution had sought refuge beyond the Roman frontiers:

'The barbarians can now boast of their own conduct when com-pared with that of the persecutors, for they received and kept in

generous captivity those who then fled from amongst us, securing
to them not merely safety, but the free exercise of their religion.
And now the Roman race bears this reproach perpetually that
those who were then driven from the Roman world found a refuge
and a home amongst the barbarians.'[74]

As a final exemplification of Constantine's activity as
bishop may be mentioned the letter from which we learn
that even before the Council of Nicaea the emperor had
placed upon the first Christian index of forbidden books
the writings of Porphyry, the foe of the Christians, an index
to which were later added the works of Arius and the
literature of the various heretical sects. The Arians in
obloquy were henceforth to be known as Porphyriani.[75]

Such is the evidence to be derived from the letters and
edicts of Constantine; its cumulative effect would appear
to me to be of considerable weight. I will not weaken that
effect by any lengthy comment. But to my mind one or
two conclusions do naturally present themselves and these
may be briefly formulated. The letters and edicts of
Constantine are not the writings of one who was merely
a philosophical monotheist whose faith was derived from
the religious syncretism of his day—a faith into which
Christianity had been absorbed. Salvatorelli's view cannot,
I believe, be maintained. The emperor has definitely identified himself with Christianity, with the Christian Church
and the Christian creed. Further, here is a sovereign
with the conviction of a personal mission entrusted to him
by the Christian God—a mission which imposes duties; it
is a charge which he cannot escape, if he would. In the
third place, in Constantine's thought the prosperity of the
Roman state is intimately, one may, I think, say necessarily,
linked to the cause of unity within the Catholic Church.
If God is to do His part, the Emperor and the Christian
Church must render to him in return—as ἀμοιβή—the
loyalty of concord. Here, I believe, is to be found the determining factor in the religious policy of the emperor—his
aim was ever to establish unity in the Catholic Church.[76]

After his failure in Africa he found the basis of union in the Homoousion of the Council of Nicaea, and that formulation of Christian doctrine he persistently and consistently maintained. He has been accused of weakness and of hesitation in the execution of his religious policy; yet in his purpose he never wavered, though he might vary the means chosen for its realization; he knew that it was idle in the cause of unity to create schism. We think of Constantine as the enemy of Athanasius. That is perhaps because we read the history of the time through the eyes of Athanasius. Constantine supported the Eusebian party because that party stood for inclusion, while Athanasius was the representative of a policy of exclusion. The Eusebians were willing to restore schismatics—the Melitians—and heretics—the Arians—when they had repented of their errors, and Athanasius was not so willing. Constantine's vision was that of a Roman Empire sustained by a Christian God and founded on an orthodox faith. That vision was ultimately realized in the New Rome which he had founded.[77] Constantine, the *religiosissimus Augustus*, has his place amongst the seers and the prophets. It was not altogether unfitting that he should be laid to rest in the Church of the Twelve Apostles, himself the thirteenth Apostle.[78]

NOTES

By the courtesy of the British Academy I have been permitted to add to my Lecture a few bibliographical notes. I hope that they may serve as an introduction to the more important modern literature on the subject.

1. A recent attempt to explain Constantine's action in this way was made by Delle Selve, *La Chiesa e Costantino il Grande*, &c., La Scuola cattolica, Anno xl, Serie 4, vol. 24 (Oct. 1912), pp. 141–63, (Nov. 1912) pp. 290–306, who wrote: 'Un uomo politico perspicace e resoluto, che sentisse e capisse altresì i bisogni e le tendenze religiose del suo tempo, non poteva fare diversamente da quanto fece Costantino' (p. 163). With such a judgement I should find it difficult to agree.

2. This fraction is nothing more than a guess, and is here used simply as such. For the consideration of the materials upon which any conjectural estimate must be based, cf. Adolf Harnack, *Die Mission und Ausbreitung des Christentums*, 4th edn., Hinrichs, Leipzig, 1924, especially his statement of results pp. 946–58, and V. V. Bolotov, *Lektsii po istorii drevnei tserkvi*, vol. 3, Merkushev, S. Peterburg, 1913, pp. 17–29.

3. On this cf. Emil Brunner, *Der Mittler. Zur Besinnung über den Christusglauben*, Mohr, Tübingen, 1927, ch. 6, *Der Christusglaube und die historische Forschung*, pp. 128–71, especially at p. 138: 'Die Weltanschauung diktiert also hier der Historie ihre Hypothesen, und die Verwechslung von moderner Weltanschauung und Wissenschaft verführt nun dazu, diese Konstruktionen oder Hypothesen darum, weil sie in die moderne Weltanschauung passen, für historisch wissenschaftlicher zu halten als die für den modernen Menschen unannehmbaren Zeugnisse des Neuen Testaments selbst.' What is true of the modern study of the New Testament holds good in other fields of research.

4. Jakob Burckhardt, *Die Zeit Constantins des Grossen*, 3rd edn., Seeman, Leipzig, 1898, p. 369 (1st edn., Basel, 1853).

5. The true title of the *Vita Constantini* of Eusebius is εἰς τὸν βίον Κωνσταντίνου: 'die Schrift . . . ein βίος weder heisst noch ist', von Wilamowitz-Moellendorf, *Ein Bruchstück aus der Schrift des Porphyrius gegen die Christen*, Zeitschrift für die neutestamentliche Wissenschaft 1 (1900), pp. 101–5, at p. 105 n.; cf. Ranke, *Weltgeschichte*, 4, 2 (1883), pp. 249–63, cited by I. A. Heikel in his edition of the *Vita* (=*Griechische Christliche Schriftsteller, Eusebius Werke*, vol. 1), Hinrichs, Leipzig, 1902, p. xlv, n. 3 (I quote from this edition throughout these notes). See the whole section of Heikel's introduction on *Zweck und Charakter der Schrift 'Über das Leben Constantins'*, ibid., pp. xlv–liii, and cf. the characterization of the work given by Paul Wendland, *Berliner philologische Wochenschrift* 22 (1902), col. 228: it is an ἐγκώμιον 'das in der Behandlung des Stoffes den deutlichen Anschluss an die Topik und die Vorschriften der Rhetoren zeigt, wenn auch die Disposition durch die Gruppierung der Thatsachen unter den Gesichtspunkt der εὐσέβεια beeinflusst ist, hochrhetorisch in Rhythmus, Hiatscheu, Periodisierung, in dem προοίμιον geradezu verkünstelt und verschnörkelt. Die Einordnung der Schrift in die fest ausgeprägte Litteraturgattung, die Einsicht in die vom Rhetor verwandten üblichen Kunstmittel ist von gleicher Bedeutung für die Characteristik des Eusebius, den man mit dem Maase seiner Zeit und ihres Geschmackes messen

muss, für die historische Verwertung der Reden und für die Text-kritik.' See further the interesting paper of C[arl] W[eyman], *Eusebius von Cäsarea und sein Leben Constantins*, Historisch-politische Blätter für das katholische Deutschland 129 (1902), pp. 873–92. P. Meyer in his short paper *De Vita Constantini Eusebiana*, published in the Festschrift dem Gymnasium Adolfinum zu Moers zu der am 10 und 11 August d. J. stattfindenden Jubelfeier seines drei-hundertjährigen Bestehens gewidmet vom Lehrerkollegium des Gymnasiums zu Crefeld, Bonn, 1882, pp. 23–8 suggests that in the *V.C.* Eusebius was answering such criticisms of Constantine's policy as we find in the second book of the *History* of Zosimus. The emperor may have himself suggested the composition of the work, and others, besides Praxagoras of Athens, may have produced similar defences.

We have gained at least some further understanding of the work of Eusebius through modern literary criticism; we should hardly write, as did Theodor Zahn in 1876, 'unter Anrufung des gött-lichen Beistands zeichnete Eusebius ein Heiligenbild dessen innere Unwahrheit und äussere Hässlichkeit in der geschichtlichen Litte-ratur ihresgleichen sucht', *Konstantin der Grosse und die Kirche*, re-printed in Skizzen aus dem Leben der Alten Kirche, 2nd edn., Deichert, Erlangen and Leipzig, 1898, pp. 209–37, at p. 210. No longer, with Brieger, should we stigmatize the *V.C.* as 'eine absichtliche Fälschung', Theodor Brieger, *Constantin der Grosse als Religionspolitiker. Kirchengeschichtlicher Essay*, Perthes, Gotha, 1880, p. 6. The more closely Eusebius is studied, the more impossible do such judgements appear. Cf. L. Salvatorelli, *La politica religiosa e la religiosità di Costantino*, Ricerche religiose 4 (1928), at pp. 325–6.

6. *Op. cit.* (see p. 31), p. 326.

7. *Ibid.*, p. 355.

8. F. Lot, *La fin du monde antique et le début du Moyen Âge*, La Renaissance du Livre, Paris, 1927, p. 34; the remark is borrowed from a note in L. Duchesne's *Early History of the Christian Church* (English translation), vol. 2, p. 48 (French: 3rd edn., vol. 2, 1908, p. 60): 'We cannot wonder too much at the artless simplicity of certain critics who approach this imperial literature with the pre-conceived idea that it was impossible for an emperor to have religious convictions, that men like Constantine, Constantius, or Julian were in reality free thinkers, who, for political exigencies, publicly proclaimed such and such opinions. In the fourth century, free-thinkers, if there were any, were *rarae aves* whose existence could not be assumed or easily accepted.' The longer a student

works with Duchesne's masterpiece in his hands, the more mysteri-
ous does the condemnation of these three magnificent volumes
appear.

9. Otto Seeck, *Die Urkunden der Vita Constantini*, Zeitschrift für
Kirchengeschichte 18 (1897), p. 332. 'Was ist also daran Auffäl-
liges, wenn auch der gute Konstantin die gleichen Trivialitäten
vorträgt?'

10. Eduard Schwartz, *Kaiser Constantin und die christliche Kirche*,
Teubner, Leipzig, 1913.

11. Cf. *ibid.*, pp. 94, 170.

12. *Ibid.*, pp. 95–6.

13. *Ibid.*, p. 149.

14. *Ibid.*, p. 155.

15. Athanasius 'hat nie aus innerem Bedürfnis zur Feder ge-
griffen; sie ist ihm stets nur ein Werkzeug seiner politischen Pläne
gewesen. Erst als streitbarer Kirchenfürst betrachtet, steigt er zu
imposanter Grösse empor' (*ibid.*, p. 159). From the early days of his
bishopric 'entwickelte er sich zu einem Hierarchen ersten Ranges'.
He marched from one triumph to another 'weil er sich nie für
unterlegen gehalten, immer an den Sieg der eigenen Sache ge-
glaubt hat. Nicht nur ein unbeugsamer Mut und die Verachtung
materieller Vorteile, sondern auch alle Mängel dieser mensch-
lich abstossenden, geschichtlich grossartigen Natur, die Mono-
tonie des Denkens und Empfindens, die Unfähigkeit, zwischen
Moral und Politik einen Unterschied zu machen, das Fehlen
jeglichen Zweifels an der eigenen Gerechtigkeit, kamen dem
stahlharten, hierarchischen Machtwillen zugute, der in ihm zum
erstenmal, seitdem es eine Kirche gab, rein und klar zum
Ausdruck kommt, sofort nachdem die Reichskirche diesem Typus
den Boden bereitet hatte' (*ibid.*, pp. 159–60). Athanasius was the
only man within the Church 'der den Mut hatte, dem Despoten
zu trotzen, und das wird immer sein Ruhm bleiben, auch wenn
nicht frommer Glaube oder die Eifer für die Selbständigkeit der
gesamten Kirche, sondern der hierarchische Stolz auf die Auto-
rität seines Patriarchats die Triebfeder dieses Mutes gewesen ist'
(*ibid.*, p. 169).

16. *Modern studies of the personality and policy of Constantine.*
   Von der Parteien Gunst und Hass verwirrt
      Schwankt sein Charakterbild in der Geschichte.

The famous lines have often been applied to Constantine; so
many religious and political prepossessions have distorted men's

portraits of the first Christian emperor. 'J'ai essayé de me faire le contemporain des temps dont je raconte l'histoire, et le plaisir que j'ai trouvé à vivre au milieu des événements du passé m'a permis de fermer l'oreille aux querelles d'aujourdhui.' How simple it sounds!—but we are soon reminded that all students are not as Gaston Boissier.

The modern reaction against Burckhardt's portrait of Constantine may be said to have begun with Theodor Keim's essay, *Der Übertritt Konstantin's des Grossen zum Christenthum*, Orell Füssli und Comp., Zürich, 1862. For Keim the religious factor is primary in Constantine's development, but religious impulses could not become convictions until the calculation, the shrewdness of the statesman had admitted their practicability and counselled their realization. It is the union of the political and religious elements in Constantine's action which makes of the emperor a figure in world history. The significance of Keim's study lies in his view that Constantine, 'der verhängnisvolle Mann dessen Schöpfung im Aufbau und Gelingen sich ganz und gar mit Religion verschlang, wirkte nicht nur für die Religion sondern *durch* Religion und in ihrem Namen und nur so wirken konnte' (quotation from p. 67, slightly adapted). Theodor Zahn's, *Konstantin der Grosse und die Kirche* (Hannover, 1876, reprinted in *Skizzen aus dem Leben der Alten Kirche*, 2nd edn., Deichert, Erlangen und Leipzig, 1898) followed after an interval of fourteen years; it still remains an important paper. In general his account of the emperor's religious development is similar to that of Keim. Both writers interpret the years after 312 as a period in which Constantine's *own thought* was definitely syncretistic—his aim the foundation of a new religion which was neither Christianity nor the traditional cult of the Roman gods, but 'die Verehrung der über allen Kulten stehenden Gottheit' (Zahn, p. 222 of reprint). Zahn can write: 'Zum Christentum hat sich Konstantin während der zehn Jahre nach dem Siege bei Rom durch keinen öffentlichen Akt bekannt . . . Als ein ausserhalb der Kirche Stehender beobachtete und behandelte er die Vorgänge innerhalb derselben' (*ibid.*, p. 223). A student who will carefully consider the whole of the emperor's correspondence during the Donatist controversy will, I believe, find it impossible to subscribe to this judgement. In France, Duruy carried to greater lengths this conception of a 'new religion' which should unite Constantine's subjects in a common worship of a supreme 'Divinitas' standing above all the historic cults. In Duruy's view Constantine never really passes beyond this conception—'à l'heure suprême il gardait donc la foi qu'il avait toujours attestée dans l'intérêt de la paix publique, la croyance à la *summa divinitas* des philosophes et des ariens'—the emperor becomes on this theory, in the words of Gaston Boissier, 'un sage dégagé de tous les préjugés de secte'. Religion was for him the statesman's secret: 'Constantin fut avant tout un politique, il vit dans la religion un moyen de gouvernement'. 'Nous avons essayé de pénétrer jusqu'au fond de l'âme de Constantin, et nous y avons trouvé une politique plutôt qu'une religion. (Duruy, *Histoire des Romains*, &c., nouvelle édition, Hachette, Paris, T. 7, 1885, pp. 36–154[1].) The theory is in the main based on the language of the 'Edict of Milan', but the document needs itself to be interpreted by reference to Constantine's action after the victory of the Milvian Bridge, if we would comprehend the personal views of the emperor—so rightly Brilliantov, *Imperator Konstantin velikii i milanskii edikt 313 goda*, Petrograd, 1916, p. 159. Constantine was no impartial deist: has Duruy never felt the passion which throbs and pulses in some of the emperor's letters? But perhaps Boissier is right after all. It may be that for our sophisticated minds the explanation which would naturally suggest itself from a reading of those letters is disappointingly obvious: Constantine 'parlait volontiers, il aimait à écrire; il semble donc que nous n'ayons, pour le connaître, qu'à étudier avec soin ce qui nous reste de lui, et que, dans ses lois, dans ses discours, dans ses lettres, nous saisirons aisément les traits principaux de sa figure. Par malheur, quand nous avons affaire à ces grands personnages, qui jouent les premiers rôles de l'histoire, et que nous essayons d'étudier leur vie et de nous rendre compte de leur conduite, nous avons peine à nous contenter des explications les plus naturelles. Parce qu'ils ont la réputation d'être des hommes extraordinaires, nous ne voulons jamais croire qu'ils aient agi comme tout le monde. Nous cherchons des raisons cachées à leurs actions les plus simples; nous leur prêtons des finesses, des combinaisons, des profondeurs, des perfidies dont ils ne sont pas avisés. C'est ce qui est arrivé pour Constantin; on est tellement convaincu d'avance que ce politique adroit a voulu nous tromper, que, plus on le voit s'occuper avec ardeur des choses religieuses et faire profession d'être un croyant sincère, plus on est tenté de supposer que c'était un indifférent, un

---

[1] In those bibliographies—the curse of modern scholarship—which merely reproduce the references given in former bibliographies, the reader will find articles by Duruy cited from *Revue Archéologique* 43 (1882), pp. 96–110, 155–75, and from *Mémoires de l'Académie des Sciences morales et politiques* (Paris) 16 (1881), pp. 737–65, 17 (1882), pp. 185–227; all these are only separate publications of sections from vol. 7 of his *Histoire des Romains*.

sceptique, qui, au fond, ne se souciait d'aucun culte et qui pré-
férait celui dont il pensait tirer les plus d'avantages' (*La Fin du
Paganisme*, 4me édition, Hachette, Paris, 1903, vol. 1, pp. 24–5).
For a criticism of Duruy see Duc de Broglie, *Deux portraits de
Constantin*, Le Correspondant N.S. 117 (153), 1888, pp. 589–611.

The leading modern representative of the view that in the years
after 312 Constantine remained in his personal thought a believer
in a religious syncretism is L. Salvatorelli. That view he has
consistently expressed: *La politica religiosa degl'imperatori romani e
la vittoria del cristianesimo sotto Costantino* in Saggi di Storia e politica
religiosa, Lapi, Città di Castello, 1914, pp. 101–24; *Rivista storica
italiana* N.S. 5 (1927), pp. 166–79; *Costantino il Grande* (in the series
Profili, No. 103), Formiggini, Roma, 1928; and in his admirable
study *La politica religiosa e la religiosità di Costantino* in Ricerche
religiose 4 (1928), pp. 289–328. Here we have the most per-
suasive presentation of the theory; I believe it to be untenable (see
Appendix *infra*), but Salvatorelli's treatment is full of suggestion.

In Germany a return to the purely political motivation of Constantine's action was marked by the pamphlet of Theodor Brieger,
Constantin der Grosse als Religionspolitiker, Perthes, Gotha, 1880
(originally appeared in the *Zeitschrift für Kirchengeschichte*, 4). This
short study is perhaps the most forceful statement of this view of
the emperor's policy.[1]

Eduard Schwartz may be regarded as the modern representative
of this standpoint. The text of my Lecture gives the reasons for
my dissent from this interpretation of Constantine's action. Despite
my profound respect for the scholarship of Schwartz, I believe
that his conception of the character and aims alike of Constantine
and Athanasius is essentially inhuman: this prodigious simplification does scant justice to the complexity of human personality.
The view that Constantine adopted in religious diplomacy as his
principle of action the Roman maxim 'divide et impera' I find
it impossible to believe; in my judgement 'der Wille zur Macht'
is not the master-key which will disclose to us all the secrets of the
life of either emperor or patriarch. For Schwartz's papers—*Zur
Geschichte des Athanasius* (see p. 50)—my admiration only grows
with the years, but with the years my doubts of his interpretation
of the personality of Constantine become more pronounced. That
interpretation should be studied in his book, *Kaiser Constantin und
die christliche Kirche*, Teubner, Leipzig, 1913, rather than in his

---

[1] For a criticism of Burckhardt and Brieger written from a Roman Catholic
standpoint, see H. Grisar, *Die vorgeblichen Beweise gegen die Christlichkeit Constantins des Grossen*, Zeitschrift für katholische Theologie 6 (1882), pp. 585–607.

article *Constantin* in *Meister der Politik*, edd. Erich Marcks and Karl Alexander von Müller, Deutsche Verlags-Anstalt, Stuttgart and Berlin, vol. 1, 1922, pp. 171–223. The latter is brilliantly written, but it carries to yet further lengths the views expressed in the book. This harsher restatement reads as a gage of challenge flung down before the critics.

G. Costa's view would appear to be formed on similar lines, but his general article on the subject published in *La Rassegna contemporanea* of 25 March 1913 is out of print and inaccessible to me. Not even the author could supply me with a copy. Costa's promised monograph—cf. *Bilychnis* 3 (1914), pp. 103–4—has not to my knowledge appeared, and the student must be content with the hints given in *Critica e tradizione. Osservazioni sulla politica e sulla religione di Costantino*, Bilychnis 3 (1914), pp. 85–105, and in his *Religione e Politica nell'impero romano*, Bocca, Torino, 1923.

At the other extreme from Burckhardt and Schwartz stands Valerian Şesan. His learned, though diffuse, work—*Kirche und Staat im römisch-byzantinischen Reiche seit Konstantin dem Grossen und bis zum Falle Konstantinopels*, vol. 1 (no more published), Bukowinaer Vereinsdruckerei, Czernowitz, 1911, is of value to West-European students, since it helps us to understand the Orthodox conception of Constantine as a Christian saint. For us West-European folk the halo of sanctity always seems to rest somewhat ambiguously on the emperor's head; his own comprehension of Christianity had a highly individual stamp, and, if a saint, we should prefer to place him amongst Usener's *Sonderbare Heilige*.[1] In Şesan's book we see a Constantine who was deemed worthy of a special divine intervention that he might become God's providential champion of the Christian Church. The Greek has construed history as Constantine himself interpreted it. In West-European scholarship the nearest approach to the spirit in which Şesan's book is written is Jules Maurice's *Constantin le Grand. L'origine de la civilisation chrétienne*, Éditions Spes, Paris, n.d., in which Constantine appears as the founder of Christian chivalry. There is no need to attempt any estimate of the value of this work; it was written after a period of great personal strain and under the impact of the war. Its main thesis cannot be sustained—this applies also to Maurice's article *La politique religieuse de Constantin le Grand*, Comptes Rendus, Académie des Inscriptions et Belles Lettres,

---

[1] The study by Ludwig Wrzoł, *Konstantins des Grossen persönliche Stellung zum Christentum*, Weidnauer Studien, published by the Priesterseminar in Weidenau (Oest.–Schlesien), Heft 1, Weidenau, 1906, pp. 227–69, is interesting as a demonstration of the limitations of the Christianity of Constantine.

1919, pp. 282–90—and the respect of scholars for his magistral *Numismatique Constantinienne* has been shown in a conspiracy of silence, unnecessarily broken by L. Salvatorelli in *Rivista storica italiana* N.S. 5 (1927), pp. 166–79.[1]

Few modern scholars knew the literature of the fourth century with such intimacy as did Otto Seeck; his portrait of Constantine as drawn in his *Geschichte des Untergangs der antiken Welt* is remarkably sympathetic when it is remembered that it was the work of one whose passionate hatred of Christianity the years failed to abate. In this picture, I feel, much of the spirit of the age has been truly caught, and Seeck brought into full relief the honesty of the emperor and his devotion to the Christian faith, as he understood it: 'alle Äusserungen seiner (Constantine's) religiösen Gesinnung finden die Modernen zweideutig, weil sie sie zweideutig finden wollen' (*Geschichte*, 2nd ed., vol. 1, 1898, p. 471)[2]. But Seeck's scorn for that faith falsifies the picture, and in my judgement he has seriously under-rated Constantine's intelligence.

Amongst the studies of Constantine with which I am personally most in sympathy may be mentioned (i) those of V. Schultze, especially *Untersuchungen zur Geschichte Konstantins des Grossen*, Zeitschrift für Kirchengeschichte 7 (1885), pp. 343–71, 8 (1886), pp. 517–42; *Quellenuntersuchungen zur Vita Constantini des Eusebius*, *ibid.*, 14 (1894), pp. 503–55; *Altchristliche Städte und Landschaften*, I, *Konstantinopel*, Deichert, Leipzig, 1913; and his article on *Konstantin der Grosse und seine Söhne* in Hauck, Realencyclopädie für protestantische Theologie, 10, pp. 757–70: 'Zweifelsohne wird die politische Seite überschätzt und wahrscheinlicher hat sie gar keine Rolle gespielt' at p. 762; (ii) the admirable study by F. X. Funk in his *Rede zum Geburtsfest des Königs 1893* (appeared originally in shorter form in *Theologische Quartalschrift*, 1896, pp. 429–62, and was republished in *Kirchengeschichtliche Abhandlungen und Untersuchungen*, Paderborn, 1899, vol. 2, pp. 1–23), *Konstantin der Grosse und das Christentum*. This has perhaps hardly received the attention which it deserves; (iii) the suggestive paper by Raffaele Mariano, *Costantino Magno e la chiesa cristiana*, Nuova Antologia di scienze, lettere ed arti, Ser. iii, vol. 27 (1890), pp. 271–99 (reprinted in vol. 5 of his *Scritti Varii*, Barbèra, Firenze, 1902, pp. 257–300), where the aim of Constantine's religious policy is, in my judge-

---

[1] The contentions of the book have been adopted without criticism by Anon. (?M. Barbera), *La politica religiosa di Costantino Magno*, La Civiltà cattolica, 1929, vol. 3, pp. 412–22.

[2] Cf. his earlier paper *Die Bekehrung Constantins des Grossen*, Deutsche Rundschau 67 (1891), pp. 73–84.

ment, very ably stated; (iv) K. Müller, *Kirchengeschichte*, vol. 1, Lieferung 2, Mohr, Tübingen, 1927 (in *Grundriss der theologischen Wissenschaften*, Abteilung 2), pp. 343–97, and cf. his article *Konstantin der Grosse und die christliche Kirche*, Historische Zeitschrift 140 (1929), pp. 261–78.

Finally, mention may be made of Pierre Batiffol's *La Paix Constantinienne et le Catholicisme*, Lecoffre, Paris, 1914, and of the pamphlet by H. Koch, *Konstantin der Grosse und das Christentum*, Mörike, München, 1913, which is mainly devoted to putting the reign of Constantine into its historical setting and sketching the issue of his action in the later history of the Church; I cannot refrain from referring as a curiosity to the 'Charakterbild' of Constantine given by J. Dräseke in *Wochenschrift für klassische Philologie*, 1908, col. 1339.

The following works are, in my judgement, of little historical importance or independent value: C. B. Coleman, *Constantine the Great and Christianity*, Columbia University Studies in History Economics and Public Law, vol. 60, no. 1. Columbia University Press, New York, 1914; K. Demetriades, *Die christliche Regierung und Orthodoxie Kaiser Konstantin des Grossen. Eine historische Studie*, Ackermann, München, 1878; F. M. Flasch, *Constantin der Grosse als erster christlicher Kaiser*, Bucher, Würzburg, 1891.

J. B. Firth's *Constantine the Great*, Putnam's, New York and London, 1905, is a readable short biography, but there is, I think, room for a fuller study of the emperor's reign written for English readers.

Modern Russian work: Russian scholarship would seem to have contributed curiously little to the study of Constantine's religious policy. V. V. Bolotov's attempt to minimize the Christian inspiration of Constantine's action, and his effort to postpone the emperor's approximation to Christianity until towards the end of his life appear to me laboured and unconvincing, *Lektsii po istorii drevnei tserkvi* (see note 2, p. 31), vol. 3, pp. 7–35. P. V. Gidulyanov has considered the conversion and religious policy of Constantine as an introduction to his work on the eastern patriarchates. He would regard religious motives as paramount in the life of the emperor and leaves it an open question how far political considerations contributed to the conversion, *Vostochnuie Patriarchi v period chetuirekh pervuikh vselenskikh Soborov*, Yaroslavl, 1908, especially at pp. 15, 19. A. A. Spassky's article on the emperor's conversion, which is frequently referred to, appeared in the *Bogoslovskii Vyestnik* for December 1904 and January 1905 (*Obrashchenie imperatora Konstantina B. v Khristianstvo*), but this journal is for me inaccessible. A. P. Lebedev's study, *Obrashchenie Konstantina*

Velikago v Khristianstvo, in vol. 9 of his collected works, 2nd edn., S.-Peterburg, 1903, pp. 30–50, is a determined defence of every detail in the Eusebian account of the Vision of the Cross. It is not, in my judgement, remarkable, and completely fails to realize the significance of the problem presented to the student by the Lactantian account of the introduction of the Christian monogram. Lebedev's essay contained in the same volume (pp. 51–82)—*Pervuii khristianskii imperator na tronye rimskikh tsezarei*—is a eulogy of Constantine which is to my mind excessive.

The one really valuable work in Russian on the subject known to me is A. Brilliantov's *Imperator Konstantin Velikii i milanskii edikt 313 goda*, Merkushev, Petrograd, 1916, in the sixth section of which there is a consideration of Constantine's general religious policy in its relation to the Edict of Milan.

17. This has been partially attempted by Johannes Maria Pfättisch in his essay *Die Kirche in den Schriften Konstantins des Grossen*, Historisch-politische Blätter für das katholische Deutschland 151 (1913), Heft 10, pp. 753–70; see also W. Hartmann, *Konstantin der Grosse als Christ und Philosoph in seinen Briefen und Erlassen*, Beilage zum Programm des städtischen Gymnasiums zu Fürstenwalde Ostern 1902, Fürstenwalde, Spree, and I. A. Heikel in the introduction to his edition (cf. note 5, p. 31): *Die religiöse Anschauung Constantins auf Grund seiner eigenen Schreiben*, pp. lxxxiii–xc. There is a brief summary of Constantine's faith from the evidence of the letters in A. Feder's article *Konstantins des Grossen Verdienste um das Christentum*, Stimmen aus Maria-Laach 84 (1913), pp. 28–43, at p. 41 (otherwise the article is unimportant).

18. (i) Documents cited in the *Vita Constantini* of Eusebius. That the documents inserted in the *Vita Constantini* are a forgery of Eusebius himself has been consistently maintained by Amedeo Crivellucci, *Della fede storica di Eusebio nella vita di Costantino*, Livorno, 1888; *I documenti della Vita Constantini*, Studi Storici 7 Giusti, (1898), pp. 412–29, 453–9. This view was adopted by Otto Seeck and criticized by Mommsen (*Constitutiones duae Cretenses*, Eph. Epigr., 1892, 7, p. 420, n. 1). Schultze declined to accept Crivellucci's view (*Theologisches Literaturblatt*, 1889, col. 81 f., 89 f.), but in 1894 rejected both the Edict to the Provincials of Palestine and the Encyclical to the Orientals [V. Schultze, *Quellenuntersuchungen zur Vita Constantini des Eusebius*, Zeitschrift für Kirchengeschichte 14 (1894), pp. 503–55, at pp. 527–41.] He suggested that they were forgeries, dating from the reign of Valentinian, intended to influence that emperor by their picture

of Constantine's policy as adapted to later conditions (pp. 537–41). The objections of Schultze were admirably answered by Crivellucci, *Gli Editti di Costantino ai Provinciali della Palestina e agli Orientali*, Studi Storici iii (1894), pp. 369–84 (on the edict to the Provincials of Palestine), pp. 415–22 (on the edict to the Orientals). Meanwhile Seeck had been led to reconsider the whole question, and had published a masterly defence of all the documents—Otto Seeck, *Die Urkunden der Vita Constantini*, Zeitschrift für Kirchengeschichte 18 (1897), pp. 321–45. A. Mancini had argued in 1895–6 that (i) Eusebius copied from his own *Church History* when writing the *Vita Constantini* (probably to be explained by the fact that the *V.C.* never received its final form; the passages copied from the *V.C.* would have been recast by Eusebius); (ii) some passages in *V.C.* which are practically the same as the text of *H.E.* are later interpolations, inserted as literary reminiscences by a reader who knew the *H.E.*, e.g. *V.C.* 1, 47, 1, compared with *H.E.* 8, 13, 15; *V.C.* 1, 33, διαζευγνύς . . . κατέχουσι secludendum (repeated in μυρίαις μὲν . . . ψυχήν) = derived from *H.E.* 8, 14, 2; (iii) there are interpolations in *H.E.* from *V.C.*—once more a reader's reminiscence of a parallel passage, e.g. *V.C.* 1, 34, inserted in *H.E.* 8, 14, 17. [A. Mancini, *Sopra talune interpolazioni nella Vita Constantini e nella Hist. Eccl. di Eusebio*, Studi Storici 4 (1895), pp. 531–41, 5 (1896), pp. 9–15.] When Heikel, in his edition of Eusebius's writings on Constantine (see note 5, p. 31), had elaborately defended the authenticity of the documents inserted in the *V.C.* (pp. lxvi–xc), Mancini published a lengthy review of that edition [*Osservazioni sulla Vita di Costantino d'Eusebio*, Rivista di filologia 33 (1905), pp. 309–60]. He contended that the documents were forgeries composed by Christians of the imperial court and chancery (p. 345) and inserted by Eusebius in the *V.C.* with knowledge of their provenance. Thus of the document reproduced in *V.C.* ii, cc. 24–42 he writes: 'Ritengo pertanto che il documento sia falso, che la falsificazione sia anteriore alla composizione della Vita e che non si debba ad Eusebio, ma che questi appunto coll'introdurlo nell'opera sua . . . abbia scientemente contribuito a far ritenere autentico un documento falso e perciò sospetto' (p. 338). This view has not, so far as I know, found any supporters. The linguistic arguments adduced by Heikel for the genuineness of the documents were reinforced in a monographic study: Alfonso Pistelli, *I documenti Costantiniani negli scrittori ecclesiastici. Contributo per la fede storica di Eusebio*, Libreria editrice fiorentina, Firenze, 1914 (criticism of Mancini, p. 70), while in the same year A. Casamassa defended at length the authenticity of the Edict to the Provincials (*I Documenti della Vita Constantini di Eusebio Cesareense* in Letture Costantiniane, &c., Desclee, Roma, 1914, pp. 1–60). The latest challenge to the authenticity of the documents is that (also published in 1914) of P. Batiffol, *Les Documents de la Vita Constantini*, Bulletin d'ancienne littérature et d'archéologie chrétiennes 4, pp. 81–95; he rejects six letters; the conclusion of his article may be quoted: 'La lettre Πεῖραν λαβών sur la fête de Pâques unifiée définit l'attitude que l'on prête à Constantin contre les Juifs; la lettre Ἐπίγνωτε νῦν définit son attitude contre les hérétiques . . .; la lettre à Sapor, Τὴν θείαν πίστιν, définit son attitude protectrice vis-à-vis des chrétiens hors de l'Empire romain;—la lettre Πάντα μὲν ὅσα, son attitude vis-à-vis des paiens;—la lettre Ἦν μὲν ἄνωθεν, son attitude vis-à-vis de l'Église;—enfin la lettre à Alexandre et à Arius, Διπλῆν μοι, son attitude vis-à-vis des Consubstantialistes et des Ariens qu'il entend réunir dans une commune indifférence aux questions oiseuses. Ces six lettres sont complémentaires les uns des autres: elles constituent un programme méthodique de politique religieuse, elles prêtent à Constantin un langage qui est fort cohérent, et qui tend à glorifier le prince, mais qui n'a rien d'historique: ces six lettres font bloc et sont une collection de faux, dont la lettre à Alexandre et à Arius trahit l'origine semiarienne, et dont la fabrication peut remonter aux environs de 340' (pp. 94–5).

This conclusion depends in part upon a view of the character of the *Vita Constantini* proposed by Jules Maurice with which must be compared the paper by G. Pasquali, *Die Composition der Vita Constantini des Eusebius*, Hermes 45 (1910), pp. 369–86. In this article Dr. Pasquali contended that the original text of the *Vita* had suffered very considerable additions and alterations. That contention has been generally admitted by scholars, but I venture to doubt whether it can be maintained. Since the question is of importance for my present purpose in this lecture it may not be out of place to attempt to justify my hesitation. In the first section of his paper Pasquali argues that the original Version of the *V.C.* did not contain the text of Constantine's letter to the Provincials. Eusebius had given in *V.C.* ii. 20–1 an analysis of the provisions of that letter, there was no need to cite it in full, and 'Nichts in der Einleitung zur Urkunde weist darauf hin, dass ein Auszug davon schon mitgeteilt worden ist; wer unbefangen liest, muss glauben, dass es sich um zwei verschiedene Gesetze handelt; und doch ist dem nicht so' (p. 376). A brief analysis of this section of the *V.C.* will best explain my own view. In c. 20 Eusebius writes ἡγοῦντο δὲ καὶ παρ' ἡμῖν, ὥσπερ οὖν καὶ πρότερον παρὰ τοῖς θάτερον μέρος τῆς οἰκουμένης λαχοῦσι, βασιλέως φιλανθρωπίας ἔμπλεοι διατάξεις, νόμοι τε τῆς πρὸς τὸν Θεὸν ὁσίας πνέοντες παντοίας παρεῖχον ἀγαθῶν ἐπαγγελίας, τοῖς μὲν κατ' ἔθνος ἐπαρχιώταις τὰ προσφορα καὶ λυσιτελῆ δωρούμενοι, ταῖς δὲ ἐκκλησίαις τοῦ θεοῦ τὰ κατάλληλα διαγορεύοντες. There follows an analysis of the provisions of these διατάξεις which constitute for the Christians the great 'liquidation' after the period of the persecutions. Then in c. 22 he proceeds δήμοις δὲ τοῖς ἐκτὸς καὶ πᾶσιν ἔθνεσιν τούτων ἕτερα ὑπερβάλλοντα τῷ πλήθει ἡ βασιλέως ἐδωρεῖτο μεγαλοψυχία, giving to the East the unprecedented privileges which the West had previously enjoyed, while (c. 23) the emperor publicly confessed that he owed his victories to the aid of the God of the Christians. Eusebius then proceeds to support these statements: μάθοις δ' ἂν τοῦ λόγου τὴν ἀρετὴν αὐτοῖς προσβαλὼν τοῖς δόγμασι; these δόγματα were two in number, τὸ μὲν ταῖς ἐκκλησίαις τοῦ θεοῦ τὸ δὲ τοῖς ἐκτὸς κατὰ πόλιν δήμοις διαπεμφθέν; he has mentioned them both previously: τοῖς μὲν κατ' ἔθνος ἐπαρχιώταις . . . ταῖς δὲ ἐκκλησίαις (see quotation above); that to the provincials he now quotes ὅ τῇ παρούσῃ προσῆκον ὑποθέσει ἔμοιγε δοκεῖ παρενθεῖναι, ὡς ἂν διὰ τῆς ἱστορίας μένοι καὶ διαφυλάττοιτο τοῖς μεθ' ἡμᾶς καὶ ἡ τοῦδε τοῦ δόγματος ἔκθεσις πρός τε ἀληθείας καὶ τῶν ἡμετέρων διηγημάτων πίστωσιν. And yet Pasquali can write; 'Nichts in der Einleitung zur Urkunde weist darauf hin dass ein Auszug davon schon mitgeteilt worden ist'. After quoting the διάταξις Eusebius proceeds with the proof of his assertions and illustrates the privileges granted δήμοις τε τοῖς ἐκτὸς καὶ πᾶσιν ἔθνεσιν: : c. 44 μεταβὰς δ' ἐκ τούτων βασιλεὺς πραγμάτων ἐνεργῶν ἥπτετο, καὶ πρῶτα μὲν τοῖς κατ' ἐπαρχίας διῃρημένοις ἔθνεσιν ἡγεμόνας κατέπεμπεν, τῇ σωτηρίᾳ πίστει καθωσιωμένους κ.τ.λ. and there follows an account of measures forbidding governors to participate in pagan sacrifices. But Eusebius has still to prove the fact of the emperor's confession that he owed his victory to the Christian God; this confession is found in Constantine's letter to Eusebius quoted in c. 46 and more particularly in the emperor's διδασκαλία ἀπελεγκτικὴ τῆς εἰδωλολάτρου πλάνης τῶν πρὸ αὐτοῦ κεκρατηκότων (c. 47) especially at c. 55. The whole section of the *Vita* is, in my judgement, carefully compiled to prove the statements made by Eusebius in his opening summary. I can see no trace of later interpolation.

Pasquali in the second section of his paper argues that in *V.C.* 1, 23, Eusebius says that he will not treat of the deaths of the persecutors; he will not τὰς τῶν ἀγαθῶν μνήμας τῇ τῶν ἐναντίων παραθέσει μιαίνειν, but later, in c. 56, he breaks his promise, and describes at length the deaths of Galerius and Maximin. 'Der Widerspruch ist augenscheinlich: wir haben noch einmal zwei Entwürfe oder doch

wenigstens die Reste zweier Entwürfe vor uns' (p. 380). But is
this inference necessary? Eusebius in writing the *V.C.* has consulted his former work—the Church History—and has begun to
copy it out. Perhaps Dr. Pasquali has never begun to copy
verbally an earlier work of his own, he has never felt the irresistible
temptation to go on copying. How good it is! we say to ourselves;
the public has never done it justice; perhaps if we reproduce it . . .
and so we are led to copy more and more. *Experto crede.* Of course,
Eusebius ought in strictness to have altered the words already
written in c. 23, but an author is not an intellectual robot[1] such as
modern criticism so often presupposes: *cuiusvis est errare.* A work
grows under an author's hand; the conception of the work changes,
as he proceeds, and he may easily fail to make the necessary conse-
quential alterations in that which he has already written. Eusebius
did not give the final polish to his encomium: granted; but can we
make any further inference? It may well be doubted.[2]

In the third section of his paper Pasquali urges that in some
chapters of the fourth book the sons of Constantine are regarded
as Caesars, in others they are already Augusti. This is, in my
judgement, simply a misunderstanding of the meaning of Eusebius.
The *V.C.* was written after the military massacre and after the
declaration as Augusti of the three sons of the dead emperor. When
Constantine died, all his three sons were absent. The body of
their captain was carried back to Constantinople by the soldiers;
there was no question of creating a new emperor; the army would
accept no one as emperor who was not Constantine's son; they
simply awaited the arrival of Constantius, and later claimed that
all three sons should be advanced from Caesars to Augusti. On
his arrival Constantius leads the funeral cortège to the Church
of the Twelve Apostles. The sentence (iv, c. 68) in which Pasquali
finds some difficulty is surely quite simple; Eusebius writes that
τὰ πανταχοῦ πάντα στρατόπεδα on hearing of Constantine's death
μίας ἐκράτει γνώμης, ὡσάνει ζῶντος αὐτοῖς τοῦ μεγάλου βασιλέως μηδένα
γνωρίζειν ἕτερον ἢ μόνους τοὺς αὐτοῦ παῖδας Ῥωμαίων αὐτοκράτορας
i.e. death had not weakened the loyalty of the troops; just as
much as if Constantine were still alive, their sole allegiance to
his family remained unshaken. It is true that Dr. Pasquali has
not made matters easier for himself by transferring (if I understand him aright) the events recounted in c. 69 from Rome to

---

[1] Cf. the unblushing confession of Mr. Bernard Shaw as quoted by Mr. St.
John Ervine in the *Observer* for 30 March 1930, p. 15.

[2] I prefer not to call in aid the hypothesis of interpolation by a reader who
knew his *Hist. Eccl.*, as would A. Mancini, *Studi Storici* 5 (1896), pp. 10–14.

Constantinople, but his difficulties are all, in my judgement, imaginary.

That Eusebius admitted some criticism of his hero into his panegyric is surely no proof of a later revision of the work. It is to some readers at least[1] one of the most refreshing features of the *V.C.* that Eusebius, the historian, is not completely silenced by the weight of the traditional form of his *laudatio*. Few modern writers have realized to the full the value of this testimony or have appreciated the intellectual probity of Eusebius which prompted him to insert these passages.[2]

In sum, I am of the opinion that Dr. Pasquali has failed to prove his case.

We turn to the arguments adduced by M. Maurice to prove 'qu'elle (the *Vita Constantini*) ait été retouchée par Eusèbe d'abord, puis dans un sens favorable à la politique de Constance II, après la mort d'Eusèbe' (*Bulletin de la Société nationale des Antiquaires de France*, 1913, pp. 387–96). The 'retouches' of Eusebius are principally to be found in the introduction and in iv, 68 where the sons of Constantine are already Augusti, while elsewhere in the *V.C.* they are still only Caesars. This, as I have tried to show, is a misapprehension of the text of Eusebius. More important are the 'additions' and 'suppressions' which are the work of the 'faussaire' of the reign of Constantius II. In *V.C.* ii, c. 44 and 45 the religious policy of Constantine is falsified; this veto upon augury and sacrifice represents the policy of Constantius II expressed in a law of 341, 'Cesset superstitio, sacrificiorum aboleatur insania'. But M. Maurice fails to point out that in this law *C. Th.* 16, 10, 2 Constantius professes that he is only renewing the legislation of his father. The force of this objection to M. Maurice's argument M. Martroye has sought to meet in his study of the meaning of the word *superstitio* in the legislation of the period (*Bulletin de la Société nationale des Antiquaires de France*, 1915, pp. 280–92). This cannot, he argues, have thus early its later meaning of pagan rites in general, but signifies superstitious practices; and the sacrifices forbidden by Constantius are accordingly those connected with superstitious practices, i.e. with divination. Thus the legislation of Constantine to which Constantius refers is that which we still possess in *C. Th.* 9, 16, 1 and 16, 10, 1. I believe that this contention cannot be maintained. M. Martroye seeks

[1] Cf. Salvatorelli (see p. 32), *Ricerche religiose* 4 (1928), pp. 325–6.

[2] Admittedly the contention urged by Dr. Pasquali in the fourth section of his paper is based upon the argument of his first section; with that argument falls the presumption on which § 4 depends.

to prove his case as follows: the first law which ordered the closing
of temples and general abstention from sacrifice is that of 1 December 354 [1] (or? 356 cf. Seeck, *Regesten*, &c., pp. 41, 40; 47, 5); in 353
Constantius abolished the nocturnal sacrifices permitted by Magnentius,[2] which is a certain proof that sacrifices were still allowed
in the day-time; therefore sacrifices could not have been forbidden
by a law of 341. In the case of the law of 354 M. Martroye's statement is simply a begging of the question; we cannot know that
C. Th. 16, 10, 4, was the first law to this effect; it *may* have only
introduced for the first time the death-penalty for the offence of
sacrifice: we cannot say. Magnentius probably permitted only
nocturnal sacrifices because he did not dare to license sacrifices
in the day-time; that is, at least, what to me the fragment of
Constantius's constitution would suggest. These constitutions will
not support the inference of M. Martroye. There follows an
examination of the use of *superstitio* in the documents previous to
the constitution of A.D. 354. In *C. Th.* 16, 10, 3 'on voit "la superstition qui doit être entièrement détruite" opposée aux édifices des
temples situés hors des murs qui doivent demeurer intacts et
préservés de toute atteinte" '. M. Martroye concludes that since
this constitution, whether of the year 346 or 342, precedes that of
354 it cannot be the pagan cult which is proscribed. But we are
told precisely why the temples outside the city-walls are to be
preserved: 'Nam cum ex nonnullis vel ludorum vel circensium vel
agonum origo fuerit exorta, non convenit ea convelli ex quibus
populo romano praebeatur priscarum sollemnitas voluptatum'. The
natural interpretation surely is that, while pagan rites are to be
suppressed, there is to be no interference with the people's pleasures.
Cf. L. Bréhier and P. Batiffol, *Les survivances du culte impérial romain*,
Picard, Paris, 1920, pp. 13–16. *C. Th.* 16, 2, 5 is referred by M.
Martroye to the superstitious usages incident to the celebration
of the recurring *lustrationes* of the Roman religion—'vieux usages
superstitieux destinés à éloigner tous les malefices, y compris la
stérilité'. He imagines that ecclesiastics were forced by their
Christian congregations to attend 'des fêtes populaires', 'des cor-
tèges se déroulant à travers la ville, bien que ces cérémonies
eussent lieu à l'occasion des sacrifices'. It is a remarkable picture.
The 'lustrum' mentioned in the constitution is doubtless the recurring celebration of a five-yearly period of an emperor's reign;
Christians had been forced by Licinius to take part in pagan rites
on the occasion of his *quinquennalia*; Constantine on the eve of the
civil war forbids any such compulsion within the Western pro-

---

[1] *C. Th.* 16, 10, 4; *C.J.* 1, 11, 1.   [2] *C. Th.* 16, 10, 5.

vinces. When Martroye interprets *C. Th.* 9, 16, 1, on the augural art, in the same way as *C. Th.* 16, 2, 5—qui superstitioni suae servire cupientes poterunt publice ritum proprium exercere—he may here be right—the words are an expression of Constantine's own aloofness from the pagan practice; but I completely fail to understand how the word *superstitio* in the Hispellum inscription can be held to have no relation to paganism: [1] 'in diesem Falle bestimmte sich der genaue Inhalt des Wortes deutlich durch den Zusammenhang, in dem es genannt, und die Lokalität auf die es bezogen wird. Die einzige Superstition, zu welcher das in Frage stehende Gebäude Veranlassung geben konnte, war der Kaiserkultus in der üblichen Form, in welcher er sich schon seit längerer Zeit fixiert hatte' (Schultze, *Zeitschrift für Kirchengeschichte* 7, pp. 364–5). The attempt to interpret *superstitio* in all these cases as meaning simply 'superstitious usages', and consequently to refer the word to the practice of divination is impossible. We must continue to believe that Constantius could refer to a law of Constantine as forbidding sacrifice. What the form of that law was we do not know, but Eusebius, we must conclude, had *some* ground for his statement, and we cannot from that statement infer that his work has been falsified.

M. Maurice further contends that the description given by Eusebius of the Labarum has been transferred to its present position in the *V.C.* by the 'faussaire' acting in the interest of Constantius. The Labarum with its representations of the Caesars is impossible in A.D. 312—the sons of Constantine only became Caesars in 317 [or ? 316]. Constantius II, as the inheritor of the Labarum, was deeply interested in his father's standard; it was therefore in the interest of Constantius that the Labarum should be carried back to an early date and associated with the vision of the Cross. This contention I am unable to disprove, but I can find nothing which can be urged in its support. It may readily be admitted that in his account of the institution of the Labarum Eusebius was in error (see p. 63), but the theory that this account stands where it does through a later interpolation appears to me to be completely arbitrary. What evidence, for instance, do we possess for the view that Constantius II was peculiarly interested in the Labarum? M. Maurice refers to the part played by Constantius in the funeral of his father; but he was the only son who could be present in the Eastern capital at the time,

---

[1] Duruy boldly maintains that in this inscription *superstitio* = Christianity; cf. *Histoire des Romains* (see p. 35), T. 7, p. 64. In this interpretation I am unable to concur.

and in the account given by Eusebius of the funeral rites there is no mention of the Labarum. The theory appears to me to be fantastic.

Finally, M. Maurice urges that the *V.C.* has been falsified in the interest of the Arian party to which Constantius II gave his support: 'Constantin y joue le rôle ridicule de pacificateur à tout prix . . . La condemnation des Ariens à Nicée est passée sous silence, le rôle d'Eustache d'Antioche est déformé, Athanase est un fauteur de troubles.' The forger has inserted, without remark, the letter of Constantine to the Council of Tyre, he openly blames 'et dans un sens arien la politique religieuse de Constantin'[1] . . . One might almost think from M. Maurice's picture that the real Eusebius was a whole-hearted supporter of Homoousian orthodoxy: if we would free ourselves from the intrusive hand of the 'faussaire' we should apparently be forced to rewrite the *Vita Constantini*. I have not the courage to attempt such a task.

M. Maurice returned to the attack in 1919 (*Bulletin de la Société nationale des Antiquaires de France*, 1919, pp. 154–5). In *V.C.* 4, 26 Eusebius speaks of Constantine's 'suppression of the importance of formulae' in wills; but this step was finally taken only after Constantine's death by the constitutions *C.J.* 6, 23, 15, and *C.J.* 2, 58, 1 of the years 339 and ? 342. We are therefore brought down to a date after A.D. 339 for the composition of the *V.C.* and perhaps to a date some years later than that. But this argument is not conclusive. In 1848 J. J. Bachofen[2] maintained that *C.J.* 6, 23, 15 and 6, 37, 21 were fragments of a single law of A.D. 339 which re-enacted the constitution of Constantine described by Eusebius. But it is probable that both these fragments are in fact wrongly dated and Seeck (*Regesten*, &c., p. 59) has suggested that *C. Th.* 8, 16 (320); 3, 2 (320); 4, 12, 3 (326); 11, 7, 3 (320); *C.J.* 6, 23, 15 (339); 6, 37, 21 (339); 6, 9, 9 and (apparently) 8, 57 (58), 1 (see Seeck, *ibid.*, p. 443) are all parts of one and the same law which was in fact issued by Constantine in the year 320. The source of the faulty dating is to be found in the fact that the years 320, 326, and 339 are all marked by imperial consulates, and such consulates are a continual source of confusion. The mention of

---

[1] A reference to *V.C.* 4, 54 which Pasquali refers to Athanasius and his supporters. But it was never contended that Athanasius was not a Christian; the charge against him was not of heresy. οἱ τὴν ἐκκλησίαν ὑποδυόμενοι καὶ τὸ Χριστιανῶν ἐπιπλάστως σχηματιζόμενοι ὄνομα must refer, in my judgement, to time-serving pagans who, to gain imperial favour, professed themselves Christians.

[2] J. J. Bachofen, *Ausgewählte Lehren des römischen Civilrechts*, Marcus, Bonn, pp. 289–91; cf. V. Schultze, *Zeitschrift für Kirchengeschichte* 14 (1894), pp. 553–5.

Serdica, in four of these fragments as the place of issue excludes, Seeck argues, the years 326 and 339. In support of this argument it should be noted that the legislation of Constantine on this subject is expressly referred to by the emperor Honorius in *C. Th.* 4, 4, 3: 'Nec enim novum promulgamus, sed divi Constantini sanctionem et inclitae recordationis sententiam patris serenitatis nostrae nostraque super huiusmodi causa quae sunt ex antiquioribus propagata secuti decreta statuimus,' &c. It will be observed that there is no mention in this constitution of any legislation on the matter issued by the sons of Constantine. We may therefore conclude that Eusebius had good grounds for his assertion.

Thus, in my judgement, neither Dr. Pasquali nor M. Maurice has proved his contention. We may still regard the *V.C.* in the form that we possess it as the work of Eusebius, though we may readily admit that it never received final revision at its author's hands. But, if this be so, the basis of Batiffol's theory of Semi-Arian interpolation is removed, while the arguments by which he sought to support that theory are, again in my judgement, quite inconclusive; I have in a later note (see p. 89) sought by the consideration of a single instance of the application of his theory to demonstrate the weakness of those arguments, and cf. Brilliantov, *Imperator Konstantin Velikii i milanskii edikt 313 goda* (see p. 40), pp. 167–71 (note), and pp. 177–9 (note).

(ii) Documents cited in Athanasius's works. Athanasius, as is well known, was for Seeck the arch-forger; the habit only grew upon him with the years—Athanasius 'im Verlauf der Jahre immer dreister in seinen Lügen wird', *Zeitschrift für Kirchengeschichte* 30 (1909), p. 419. For Seeck's charges cf. *Untersuchungen zur Geschichte des Nicänischen Konzils*, Zeitschrift für Kirchengeschichte 17 (1896), pp. 1–71, 319–62; *Urkundenfälschungen des 4. Jahrhunderts*, II, *Die Fälschungen des Athanasius, ibid.*, 30 (1909), pp. 399–433 in which he upheld his views on Athanasian forgeries expressed in his former article. As a crucial instance of his theory Seeck regarded the letter by which Constantine is alleged to have summoned to Constantinople the bishops who had condemned Athanasius at the Council of Tyre; for a defence of that letter cf. N. H. Baynes, *Athanasiana*, Journal of Egyptian Archaeology 11 (1925), at pp. 61–5, and my remarks in *Journal of Roman Studies* 18 (1928), at pp. 220–1. Further as against Seeck's contentions, cf. Sigismund Rogala, *Die Anfänge des arianischen Streites* (= Forschungen zur Christlichen Literatur- und Dogmengeschichte, edd. A. Ehrhard and J. P. Kirsch, Bd. 7, Heft 1), Schöningh, Paderborn,

1907; and see Adolf Lichtenstein, *Eusebius von Nikomedien*, &c., Niemeyer, Halle, 1903; J. M. Pfättisch, *Zur Anfangsgeschichte des arianischen Streites*, Historisch-politische Blätter für das katholische Deutschland, 144 (1909), pp. 596–612. For the study of the Athanasian Corpus the essential articles are those of E. Schwartz, *Zur Geschichte des Athanasius*, Nachrichten von der Königl. Gesellschaft der Wissenschaften zu Göttingen, Phil.-hist. Klasse, 1904, pp. 333–401; 518–47; 1905, pp. 164–87, 257–99; 1908, pp. 305–74; 1911, pp. 367–426. I desire to repeat here that it was in ignorance of the last instalment of this series that I wrote my own study of the recall of Arius from exile, *Journal of Egyptian Archaeology* 11 (1925), at pp. 58–61. I withdraw the views there expressed in favour of the reconstruction of Schwartz, cf. *Journal of Roman Studies* 18 (1928), p. 221, the more readily as it restores our confidence in the trustworthiness of Athanasian chronology. I hope to reinforce this shortly by a study of Epiphanius's account of the history of the Melitian schism: cf. *Journal of Roman Studies, ibid.*, pp. 221–2. In justification of the general attitude towards the documents adopted in this lecture I would add that after prolonged study of Seeck's articles I am convinced that Athanasius was no forger. He was a skilful advocate, and all his historical works must be judged from this standpoint. He will suppress those parts of a document which do not serve his purpose, but he was far too shrewd to forge evidence and thus to lay himself open to a damaging refutation. The lawyer in me is sincerely impressed by the ability of Athanasius; he might have been, had he desired it, a distinguished member of the Roman bar.

(iii) For documents connected with the Donatist controversy see note, p. 75. For the theory of fifth-century interpolations see the next note.

19. The *Oratio ad Sanctos* is a work of extreme difficulty; to one scholar it appears as 'eine schlecte Flickarbeit'—Ivar A. Heikel, *Kritische Beiträge zu den Constantin-Schriften des Eusebius*, &c., Texte und Untersuchungen zur Geschichte der altchristlichen Literatur, 3 Reihe, 6 Band, 4 Heft (1911), p. 16; to another 'ein Meisterwerk dessen strenge Logik im ganzen wie im einzelnen von einem kundigen Literaten zeugt'—Johannes M. Pfättisch, *Des Eusebius Pamphili vier Bücher über das Leben des Kaisers Konstantin und des Kaisers Konstantin Rede an die Versammlung der Heiligen*, &c. (in the Bibliothek der Kirchenväter), Kösel, Kempten und München, 1913, p. xvi. It offers to the student a whole series of problems to which directly contradictory answers have been given by modern writers. In this note I cannot, of course, attempt any detailed

discussion of those problems; I can only refer to the widely scattered literature upon the subject.

(i) The Argument of the *Oratio* as a whole. For a denial that there is any such consistent argument cf. I. A. Heikel, *op. cit.*, who gives a lengthy analysis of the work accompanied by a devastating commentary (pp. 2–47). J. M. Pfättisch in his monograph on the *Oratio—Die Rede Konstantins des Grossen an die Versammlung der Heiligen auf ihre Echtheit untersucht* = Strassburger Theologische Studien, edd. A. Ehrhard and E. Müller, Bd. 9, Heft 4, Herder, Freiburg, 1908—traced a considered argument throughout the address, save that he thought that the Sibylline acrostic was an addition to the original text inserted by the Greek translator.[1] This interpretation of the *Oratio* was unfortunately based upon a misconception of the phrase κόσμος φύσεως ἡ κατὰ φύσιν ζωή [*Oratio*, 1, 2, Heikel, p. 154, 12. On this phrase, cf. Stiglmayr, *Zeitschrift für katholische Theologie*, 33 (1909), p. 347, n. 2; Heikel, *Kritische Beiträge* (see *supra*), pp. 4–5; E. Schwartz, *Deutsche Literaturzeitung*, 1908, col. 3098.] A fresh and much improved analysis was published by Pfättisch in *Die Rede Konstantins an die Versammlung der Heiligen* in Konstantin der Grosse und seine Zeit, Gesammelte Studien, Festgabe zum Konstantins-Jubiläum 1913 und zum goldenen Priesterjubiläum von Mgr. Dr. A. de Waal, &c., ed. Franz Jos. Dölger (= Supplementheft der Römischen Quartalschrift 19), Herder, Freiburg, 1913, pp. 96–121; and a third analysis in schematic form was given by him in his translation of the *Oratio* (*Bibliothek der Kirchenväter*, see *supra*), pp. xvii–xx. For Eduard Schwartz the *Oratio* is an apologia for the lex divina, i.e. Christianity, and thus a justification of Constantine's own policy. It is Constantine's victory which concludes the series of proofs justifying that rational monotheism through which Emperor and Church should rule the world. *Deutsche Literaturzeitung*, 1908, col. 3098.

(ii) Is the *Oratio* a forgery? The modern discussion of the *Oratio* begins with Jean-Pierre Rossignol's book, *Virgile et Constantin le Grand*, Delalain, Paris, 1845. He maintained that the work was a forgery of Eusebius; he promised to prove the point at length in a second volume, but this was never published. A. Mancini, arguing from the form of the acrostic (with the Σταυρός strophe added) as compared with the shorter version quoted by Augustine,[2]

---

[1] F. J. Dölger considers it to be impossible to decide whether Constantine or the translator inserted the acrostic; if the latter, then the addition was made within the Constantinian period: IΧΘΥC, vol. 1, Rome, 1910, at p. 56.

[2] For Augustine's treatment of the Sibylline oracles, cf. Karl Prümm, *Das*

De Civ. Dei, 18, 23, contended that the *Oratio* was a forgery of the
second half of the fifth century—*La pretesa Oratio Constantini ad
Sanctorum Coetum*, Studi Storici 3 (1894), pp. 92–117, 207–27, and
cf. his note *Sull'acrostico della Sibilla Eritrea*, Studi italiani di filologia classica 4 (1896), pp. 537–40.[1] Heikel agreed with Mancini's
conclusion[2]: see the Preface to his edition, p. cii.[3] A. Kurfess in
Das Akrostichon Ἰησοῦς Χρειστὸς Θεοῦ Ὑιὸς Σωτὴρ Σταυρός, Sokrates
6 (1918), pp. 99–105, suggested that the Σταυρός strophe of the
acrostic was added by the Greek translator as fitting to a Good
Friday homily; cf. *Oratio*, c. 1, on which see Heikel, *Kritische
Beiträge* (see *supra*), p. 4. Paolo Fabbri, *L'ecloga quarta e Costantino
il Grande*, Historia 4 (1930), pp. 228–35, at pp. 230–1, apparently
considers that these verses may have been an addition inserted at
some date later than Augustine. Mancini's argument is, in my
judgement, quite inconclusive; there may well have been two versions of the acrostic current in the fourth century—the Σταυρός
addition has no necessary connexion with the preceding strophes.

Josef Stiglmayr—*Zur Rede Konstantins an 'die Versammlung der
Heiligen'*, Zeitschrift für katholische Theologie 36 (1912), pp. 865–8
—abandoning his former view *ibid.*, 33 (1909), pp. 346–52—infers
from Jerome's *Epistola ad Paulinum Presbyterum* (*C.S.E.L.* 54, 442–
65 at p. 453) that the *Oratio* must have been produced at a date
later than this letter, or otherwise Jerome in his polemic against
the Christian interpretation of Virgil must have referred to it.
Pfättisch has sought to meet this argument by contending that
Jerome was only criticizing the composition of Christian centos
drawn from Virgil's poems: cf. J. M. Pfättisch, *Die vierte Ekloge
Vergils in der Rede Konstantins an die Versammlung der Heiligen*, Programm des Kgl. Gymnasiums im Benediktinerkloster Ettal für das
Schuljahr 1912–13, F. X. Seitz, München, pp. 86–8. But in any
event it might be urged that it would have been imprudent for
Jerome to mention expressly the work of the first Christian emperor:

*Prophetenamt der Sibyllen in kirchlicher Literatur mit besonderer Rücksicht auf die
Deutung der 4. Ekloge Virgils*, Scholastik 4 (1929), at pp. 67–76, and see J. M.
Pfättisch, *Der prophetische Charakter der vierten Ekloge Vergils bis Dante*, Historisch-
politische Blätter für das katholische Deutschland 139 (1907), pp. 637–46,
734–51.

[1] Mancini's *Conjectanea*, in which there is apparently a further treatment of
the subject, I have been unable to procure.

[2] In Heikel's discussion of the problem Adolf Harnack found 'auch nicht
ein wirklich beachtenswertes, geschweige zwingendes Argument' against the
authenticity of the *Oratio*, *Die Chronologie der altchristlichen Litteratur*, II, ii (1904),
pp. 116–17.

[3] For composition in 5th or 6th century see J. Dräseke, *Wochenschrift für
klassische Philologie*, 1908, coll. 1339–44.

those conversant with Christian literature would supply the missing reference.

The arguments for conscious forgery, it is generally admitted, have failed to carry conviction.

(iii) But if the *Oratio* is a document of the Constantinian period, how far can it be regarded as the emperor's own composition? Eduard Schwartz boldly accepts—in the full sense of the word—Constantine's personal authorship of the whole work. The *Oratio* presents the emperor's individual conception of Christianity which is constant and did not undergo any essential development: 'denn in seinem Mittelpunkt steht die Alleinherrschaft des Kaisers selbst, die von Gott gewollt ist und in der der Sieg der Kirche gipfelt.' *Deutsche Literaturzeitung*, 1908, col. 3098; cf. Kroll-Pauly-Wissowa, *Realencyclopädie*, art. Eusebios, 6 (1907), col. 1427. Pfättisch (in 1908) in his monographic treatment of the *Oratio* thought that the directly 'Constantinian' parts of the address could be distinguished from the sections contributed by the scholar who adapted the material supplied him by the emperor. This view he later abandoned; in the *Oratio* we have: 'eine Umarbeitung der kaiserlichen Rede die von einem platokundigen Griechen besorgt wurde'; the whole is 'durchaus einheitlich konzipirt', and it is therefore impossible to separate what belongs to Constantine from the handiwork of the redactor—*Platos Einfluss auf die Rede Konstantins an die Versammlung der Heiligen*, Theologische Quartalschrift 92 (1910), pp. 399–417. Hartmann in an appendix to his study *Konstantin der Grosse als Christ und Philosoph*, &c. (see note 17, p. 40), held that 'die häufige Übereinstimmung' in the *Oratio* 'mit den Briefen spricht dafür dass Konstantin thatsächlich ... eine Rede ähnlichen Inhalts verfasst hat die dann von einem gelehrten Theologen lateinisch ausgearbeitet wurde', possibly by Lactantius.[1] On account of this 'Überarbeitung' it cannot be used as direct evidence for the thought of Constantine. P. Wendland in a valuable discussion of the *Oratio* maintained that it is, as Eusebius says (cf. *V.C.* 4, 29, 3), 'eine Predigt in Form eines Sendschreibens an die Kirche'. 'Von Eusebius', he continues, 'kann m. E. die Rede als Ganzes ebensowenig herrühren wie von Konstantin. Aber ich glaube, dass sie von einem literarischen

---

[1] Cf. V. Schultze, *Quellenuntersuchungen zur Vita Constantini des Eusebius*, Zeitschrift für Kirchengeschichte 14 (1894), pp. 542–50 where it is sought to prove that 'die Osterrede ruht in der Hauptsache auf den Schriften des Lactantius'. Heikel in his introduction would limit this dependence, pp. xciv–xcv, but cf. K. Prümm in *Scholastik* (see p. 51, n. 2), 4 (1929), pp. 64–7. 'Zeitlich und auch sonst in mehr als einer Beziehung steht Laktanz am nächsten Konstantin der Grosse', Pfättisch, *Historisch-politische Blätter*, &c. 139 (see p. 52, n.), p. 642.

Berater des Kaisers nach dessen Anleitung verfasst und unter Konstantins Namen verbreitet ist als ein Mittel der Propaganda für eine Art Christentum das die Heiden anziehen und leicht gewinnen konnte.' *Berl. phil. Woch.* 22 (1902), coll. 229–32. Similarly V. Schultze concludes that the sermon implies such a 'rhetorische Gewandheit und philosophische Bildung' as Constantine certainly never possessed. The 'translation' of which Eusebius speaks (*V.C.* 4, 32) must be taken to include 'Umarbeitung' and 'Erweiterung'. A Greek author has 'breit entfaltet' the thought of Constantine, 'und ganze Abschnitte eingelegt hat'. Eusebius may well have known the sermon in this form. *Zeitschrift für Kirchengeschichte* 14 (1894), pp. 550–1. See further A. Harnack, *op. cit.* (see note 2 on p. 52), p. 117; F. J. Dölger, *op. cit.* (see p. 51, n. 1), p. 56; K. Prümm, *Scholastik* 4 (1929), at pp. 66–7. With the view of Wendland I desire to associate myself.

(iv) The question whether the *Oratio* was originally written in Latin has been much discussed. For the affirmative, cf. Hartmann, *Konstantin der Grosse als Christ und Philosoph* (*supra* note 17, p. 40), in the Appendix on the *Oratio*; Ed. Schwartz on Latinisms in the Greek text, Kroll-Pauly-Wissowa, *Realencyclopädie*, 6, col. 1427; *Deutsche Literaturzeitung*, 1908, col. 3097; for the negative Stiglmayr in *Zeitschrift für katholische Theologie* 33 (1909), pp. 349–51, and cf. I. A. Heikel: 'admonendum videtur, ea re, quod oratio illa quaedam latini sermonis vestigia prae se fert, nullo modo demonstrari, eam re vera latina fuisse scriptam et postea in graecam linguam translatam. Nam rhetor, qui orationem composuit, sine dubio etiam latinos auctores adhibuit, ut Vergilium, et ipsius Constantini scripta. Sed versiones graecas ex latina lingua factas quisquis lectitaverit et aure calluerit, non dubitabit, quin illa oratio sit exemplar vere graecum, quamvis putidum et a Constantini scribendi genere tortuoso quidem sed nervoso plane alienum.' *De Constantini imperatoris scriptis edendis,* Inbjudning-Skrift, University of Helsingfors, dated 29 March 1916, p. 6. In particular there is acute disagreement on the questions whether the commentary on the Fourth Eclogue was originally written in Latin; whether that commentary was made upon the Latin text or Greek translation. Gerhard Rauschen maintained that the commentary was originally written in Greek; it may have been made from the Latin text by the same man who produced the Greek translation. *Literarische Rundschau für das katholische Deutschland* 36 (1910), coll. 68–70. Pfättisch has consistently urged that the commentary was first written in Latin and on the Latin text: cf. in particular his Programm of 1912–13 (see p. 52), pp. 83–4 (with this G. Loeschke agreed, *Berliner philologische Wochenschrift*, 1910, coll. 357–9); and so, independently, A. Kurfess, *Observatiunculae ad P. Vergili Maronis eclogae quartae interpretationem et versionem graecam*, Mnemosyne 40 (1912), pp. 277–84, at p. 282, who further illustrated his view by a special study of the extremely difficult commentary upon the closing lines of the eclogue, *Der Schluss der vierten Ekloge Vergils in Kaiser Konstantins Rede an die Heilige Versammlung*, Pastor Bonus, 1920–21, pp. 55–60; cf. P. Fabbri, *Historia* 4 (1930), at pp. 229–30. Pfättisch (Programm, p. 83) would admit, however, that the translation is in two places itself influenced by the commentary (vv. 7, 28–30); Kurfess would only allow the existence of a single passage where it is certain that it is the Greek text which forms the basis of the commentary; here (Heikel, p. 186, 21) we must infer, he concludes, 'Überarbeitung', *Vergils vierte Ekloge in Kaiser Konstantins Rede an die Heilige Versammlung*, Jahresberichte des philologischen Vereins zu Berlin, in Sokrates 8 (1920), pp. 90–6, at p. 94.[1]

I have read these discussions of the commentary with painful diligence; for my own part I find it difficult to arrive at any certain conclusion. I should incline to the view that the commentary was made on the Latin text of the eclogue, and that the Greek translation is an addition by another and a later hand. But it will be more honest to set down in print the humiliating truth: when one cannot translate a commentary, it is not easy to determine whether the commentator is obscuring the Latin original or a Greek version of the original text.

(v) Does the *Oratio* imply a direct use of Plato? The Platonic passages in the sermon were studied by Rossignol, *op. cit.* (see p. 51), pp. 263–302, and direct dependence upon Plato is maintained by Pfättisch in his monograph and in his article (see p. 53) in the *Theologische Quartalschrift* 1910. Such direct dependence is denied by Schwartz: the sources of the Platonism of Constantine are to be found in the apologetic works of Eusebius, *Deutsche Literaturzeitung*, 1908, col. 3098; similarly G. Loeschke in *Berliner philologische Wochenschrift*, 1910, coll. 357–9 at col. 358. Heikel sees no reason for this denial, preface to his edition, p. xcv, but cf. the note on p. xcvi. Kurfess points out that it is only from the *Timaeus* that any considerable borrowings are made, and suggests the use by Constantine of Cicero's Latin translation of that dialogue, *Platos Timaeus in Kaiser Konstantins Rede an die Heilige Versammlung*, &c., Zeitschrift für die neutestamentliche Wissenschaft, &c., 19

---

[1] A further reference may be made to A. Kurfess, *Berliner philologische Wochenschrift* ,1918 ,coll. 760–1, and *Philologische Wochenschrift*, 1930, coll. 366–8.

(1919–20), pp. 72–81. To my mind the serious objection lies in Heikel's statement, 'Der Versuch bei Constantin Platonische Gedanken aufzuspüren ist vergeblich gewesen'. *Texte und Unter-suchungen* (see p. 50), p. 23.

(vi) If the *Oratio* is Constantinian, what is its date of composition? Pfättisch has consistently argued that it is pre-Nicene; Schwartz definitely pronounces it post-Nicene. Kurfess in a special study of the problem of date would assign it to Easter 313, *Kaiser Konstantins Rede an die Versammlung der Heiligen*, Pastor Bonus 41 (1930), pp. 115–24, and to the same year P. Fabbri in *Historia* (see p. 52).

I should like to have been able to have made use of the *Oratio* in this lecture, but the fact that there are echoes of Constantine's thought in the sermon is insufficient to justify such a course when it also contains so much which is without any parallel in Constantine's unquestioned writings. I cannot believe in the emperor's 'persönliche Autorschaft' (Schwartz) of the whole, and since, with Pfättisch, I cannot distinguish between the work of Constantine and that of the redactor, I feel that it is fairer, for my present purpose, to leave the whole document strictly out of account. That there was an original Latin address of the emperor's is, in my view, practically certain; that it should have been composed after A.D. 323 without any reference to Licinius, despite the fact that Maxentius and Maximin are both, in my judgement, held up to obloquy, I regard as incredible. An adaptation of the Latin sermon was later made, I believe, by a Greek rhetorician—not, as Hartmann, by a Christian theologian—to serve in the emperor's propaganda for the conversion of the pagans. The student of Christian apologetic must give to the *Oratio* prolonged consideration; the student of Constantine's personal convictions must exercise self-denial.

20. *Cf. J. Maurice*, Numismatique Constantinienne, vol. ii, Leroux, Paris, 1911, Introduction, c. i, *La dynastie héracléenne dans l'empire des Gaules*, pp. xi–xix.

21. Cf. N. H. Baynes, *Two Notes on the Great Persecution*, The Classical Quarterly 18 (1924), pp. 189–94, *The Fourth Edict—A Suggestion*, at pp. 189–93.

22. Cf. N. H. Baynes, *ibid.*, at p. 193.

23. For Jupiter and Hercules on coin types, *Revue Archéologique*, 4me Série, T. 17 (1911), p. 382; for the highly significant evidence of the panegyrici, cf. R. Pichon, *Les derniers écrivains profanes*, Leroux, Paris, 1906, pp. 99–102, *id., La Politique de Constantin*

d'après les Panegyrici Latini, Comptes Rendus, Académie des Inscriptions et Belles Lettres, Paris, 1906, pp. 289–97, and see J. Maurice, *Les Discours des Panegyrici Latini et l'évolution religieuse sous le règne de Constantin*, *ibid.*, 1909, pp. 165–79, especially at pp. 166–7.

24. J. Maurice, *Comptes Rendus* (as in note 23), 1909, at pp. 167–70; *id.*, *La dynastie solaire des seconds Flaviens* in the Introduction to vol. ii of *Numismatique Constantinienne* (see note 20), pp. xx–xlviii; *id.*, same title, *Revue archéologique*, 4me Série, T. 17 (1911), pp. 377–406; Pichon, *Les derniers écrivains profanes* (see note 23), pp. 93–8. For the significance of this Claudian descent for the writer(s) of the *Historia Augusta*, cf. N. H. Baynes, *The Historia Augusta: its date and purpose*, Oxford, Clarendon Press, 1926, especially pp. 53 sqq.

25. Constantine's first conversion, cf. P. Batiffol, *Les étapes de la conversion de Constantin*, I, Bulletin d'ancienne littérature et d'archéologie chrétiennes 3 (1913), at pp. 179–83. For sun-worship, cf. the articles of Maurice quoted in note 24; for the sun-worship of the Danubian provinces, J. Toutain, *Les cultes païens dans l'empire romain*, I, Leroux, Paris, 1907, p. 319; for the eastern elements (Aurelian's cult of Sol Invictus, &c.), it will suffice to refer to F. Cumont, *Les religions orientales dans le paganisme romain*, 4th edition, Geuthner, Paris, 1929, especially at pp. 105–6, 122–4, 136, 270; *id.*, *After Life in Roman Paganism*, Yale University Press, 1922 at pp. 100 sqq., and his memoir, *La théologie solaire du paganisme romain*, Mémoires présentés par divers savants, Académie des Inscriptions et Belles Lettres, Paris, 12 (1913), 2me partie, pp. 447–79; G. Wissowa, *Religion und Kultus der Römer*, Beck, München, 1912 (2nd edn.), pp. 365–8 (where note particularly the contrast between the sun-cults of Elagabal and Aurelian); Franz Boll, *Die Sonne im Glauben und in der Weltanschauung der alten Völker* (= Astronomische Schriften des Bundes der Sternfreunde, No. 3), Stuttgart, 1922. For Constantine, cf. Theodor Preger, *Konstantinos-Helios*, Hermes 36 (1901), pp. 457–69, and for Julian the Apostate the section on *Un sanctuaire de Mithra*, in J. Bidez, *La Vie de l'empereur Julien*, Les Belles Lettres, 1930, pp. 219–24, and G. Mau, *Die Religionsphilosophie Kaiser Julians*, &c., Teubner, Leipzig, 1907–8, *Die Rede auf den König Helios*, pp. 3–89, 127–51, and see *infra* Appendix, pp. 95–103. For the birthday of the Unconquered Sun, cf. Boll, *Griechische Kalender*, in the *Sitzungsberichte* of the Akademie der Wissenschaften, phil.-hist. Klasse Heidelberg, 1910, Abh. 16, at pp. 40–4, and F.Cumont, *Le Natalis*

Invicti, Comptes Rendus, Académie des Inscriptions et Belles Lettres, 1911, pp. 292–8.

26. E. Schwartz has suggested that Constantine was in large measure responsible for the issue of this edict of toleration. M. Sulzberger would apparently go even further than this; he writes —*Byzantion* 2 (1925, published 1926), pp. 408–9—'Cet édit est très étrange: les empereurs énumèrent leurs griefs contre les chrétiens, avec amertume, puis leur accordent pleine liberté, et leur demandent, en retour, de prier leur Dieu pour les empereurs et le peuple. On dirait d'un édit de *persécution* de Galère (alors très malade; il devait mourir le 5 mai [whence is this date derived?], qui aurait été achevé en sens tout contraire par Constantin. *Ainsi* [the italics are mine] Constantin était, dès 311, nettement favorable aux chrétiens.' I know of no evidence in support of this view, and the silence of Eusebius is for me conclusive. If Eusebius could have claimed the participation of his hero, he would surely have stated that claim. Galerius, embittered by the failure of his religious policy, is struck down with a mortal disease. He seeks to placate the God whose anger he has provoked. This explanation of the publication of the edict given by contemporaries I accept. [Cf. J. R. Knipfing, *Revue belge de Philologie et d'Histoire*, 1 (1922), at pp. 693–5.]

27. Here the evidence of the coinage is decisive: see J. Maurice, in the *Bulletin de la Société nationale des Antiquaires de France*, 1900, pp. 314–17.

28. Cf. Otto Seeck and Georg Veith, *Die Schlacht am Frigidus*, Klio 13 (1913), pp. 451–67; N. H. Baynes, in *History* 14 (1930), at pp. 292–3.

29. Eusebius, *V.C.* 1, 26 sqq.

30. Cf. Felix Haase, *Altchristliche Kirchengeschichte nach orientalischen Quellen*, Harrasowitz, Leipzig, 1925, p. 160, note.

31. Objective reality? Cf. F. Kampers, *Vom Werdegange der abendländischen Kaisermystik*, Teubner, Leipzig, 1924, pp. 172–3, and for the appearance in S. England of the cross athwart the sun, cf. the correspondence in *The Times*, 1 April 1929, p. 11 e; 2nd, p. 8 d; 3rd, p. 8 c; 4th, p. 8 d; 6th, p. 6 g; 8th, p. 8 c; 9th, p. 12 e. For the cross at a time when the sun was high in the sky see letter of Louis Cobbett in *The Times* for 8 April 1930; for Constantine, letter of Ernest Gardner, *The Times* for 3 April, p. 13 e.

32. There will never be agreement whether or no an objective miracle was performed by God to procure Constantine's conver-

sion—never at least until the outlook on the universe of all men becomes identical. The rationalist may proclaim, 'An die berüchtigte Vision des Kaisers . . . glaubt heutzutage kein Mensch mehr' (L. Jeep, *Zur Geschichte Konstantin des Grossen*, in Historische und philologische Aufsätze Ernst Curtius . . . gewidmet, Berlin, 1884, pp. 79–95), but, of course, the statement is false; Seeck may judge the emperor's story to be 'natürlich erlogen' (*Geschichte des Untergangs der antiken Welt*, I, 2nd edn., p. 491), but Knöpfler will with the same confidence pronounce the Eusebian account to be 'Wirklichkeit und Wahrheit' see his article on *K.'s Kreuzesvision* in Historisch-politische Blätter &c. 141 (1908), pp. 183–99; while miracle can itself be denied on Christian grounds—the unworthiness of Constantine (Keim, *Übertritt*, p. 2, see p. 34), the Crucified would never have bidden the emperor use His cross as battle-charm (Zahn, *Constantin der Grosse und die Kirche*, p. 219, see p. 34).   And between the two extremes of direct affirmation and direct denial stand those who accept the *subjective* truth of the narrative, but consider that its *objective* truth is insufficiently accredited: so C. Weyman, *Eusebius von Cäsarea und sein Leben Constantins*, Historisch-politische Blätter &c., 129 (1902), pp. 873–92.   It would serve no useful purpose to multiply citations in this note : it will suffice to quote a few modern representative treatments of the subject.   From the Roman Catholic side for objective miracle, cf. F. Savio, *La guerra di Costantino contro Massenzio e le apparizioni miracolose della Croce e del Salvatore*, Civiltà cattolica, Ann. 64, vol. 2, pp. 11–32; *id.*, *Le innovazioni radicali legislative di Costantino confermano la verità delle apparizioni*, ibid., pp. 385–402; *id.*, *Le realtà delle apparizioni confermata dalle dichiarazioni solenni di Costantino*, ibid., pp. 556–73, together with the supplementary studies *Costantino Magno e la libertà cristiana*, ibid., pp. 662–73, vol. 3, pp. 129–43, and *Costantino Magno e la moralità cristiana*, ibid., pp. 397–409, 677–91.[1]   For the Orthodox Church, Valerian Şesan, *Kirche und Staat*, &c. (see p. 37), pp. 337–48. From the intermediate standpoint may be cited the fine essay by F. X. Funk, *Kirchengeschichtliche Abhandlungen und Untersuchungen*, Schöningh, Paderborn, 1899, pp. 1–23 (see p. 38), and the admirable discussion of miracle by H. Schrörs in his *Konstantins des Grossen Kreuzerscheinung, eine kritische Untersuchung*, Hanstein, Bonn, 1913, and cf. his defence against criticism in *Zur Kreuzerscheinung Konstantins des Grossen*, Zeitschrift für katholische Theologie 40 (1916), pp. 485–523; *Die Bekehrung Konstantins des Grossen in der Überlieferung*, ibid., pp. 238–57.

[1] Fedele Savio, *L'apparizione della Croce e la conversione di Costantino Magno*, Befani, Roma, 1913, is apparently a reprint of these articles.   I have not seen the book.

It is not my purpose in this place to discuss the evidence, but I desire merely to state my view (i) that it is uncritical to reject the evidence of Lactantius in favour of the account given by Eusebius—so Schrörs—and (ii) that Eusebius and Lactantius cannot be describing the same event; that the many attempts which have been made to harmonize their accounts are therefore foredoomed to failure. I need only refer further to two recent discussions: that of V. Bolotov, who thinks that Eusebius misunderstood Constantine—the emperor was not a man to welcome the questions of an interviewer! (*Lektsii po istorii drevnei tserkvi*, iii, pp. 7–16) and that of Brilliantov, *Imperator Konstantin Velikii i milanskii edikt 313 goda*, pp. 12–31 (see note 16, p. 40), and cf. the next note. The accounts of the Vision have been conveniently published in J. B. Aufhauser's *Konstantins Kreuzesvision* (= Hans Lietzmann's *Kleine Texte*, No. 108), Weber, Bonn, 1912.

33. For the purpose of this lecture it is fortunately unnecessary for me to discuss at length the origin and significance of the Labarum and the Constantinian monogram; it will suffice to mention some recent studies of the problems connected therewith. For the presumed pagan antecedents of monogram and labarum V. Gardthausen's *Das alte Monogramm*, Hiersemann, Leipzig, 1924, forms a valuable repertory (pp. 73–107). Gardthausen would, it seems, date the adoption by Constantine of the Labarum to the year 312, but regards it as 'die Sonnenfahne des von ihm seit seiner Kindheit verehrten Sonnenkultus' (p. 84). The Labarum was thus originally a 'kaiserliches', 'weltliches' standard which the Christians were permitted to interpret as a Christian symbol (p. 98). A similar theory of the origin of the Christian monogram has been maintained by G. Costa: he would regard it as derived from the symbolism of the solar religion of the Gauls, see his article *Critica e Tradizione. Osservazioni sulla politica e sulla religione di Costantino*, Bilychnis, 3, Anno 1914, 1 Semestre (February 1914), pp. 85–105 at pp. 88–95. In a frequently cited paper—*Zur Geschichte Constantin des Grossen* published in Historische und philologische Aufsätze Ernst Curtius . . . gewidmet, Asher, Berlin, 1884, pp. 79–95—Ludwig Jeep contended that both Labarum and monogram were originally pagan. This essay would appear to me to be singularly lacking in critical judgement. Similar views were expressed by A. Crivellucci in *L'origine della leggenda del monogramma e del labaro*, Studi Storici 2 (1893), pp. 88–104, 222–60.

For the Christian significance of the Labarum and its adoption in A.D. 312 Pio Franchi de' Cavalieri's very able study *Il labaro descritto da Eusebio* in Studi Romani 1 (1913), pp. 161–88 should be consulted; cf. *id., Ancora del labaro descritto da Eusebio, ibid.*, 2 (1914), pp. 216-23. His contentions and arguments have been approved and illustrated by Joseph Wilpert in his lecture *Vision und Labarum Konstantins des Grossen im Licht der Geschichte und Archäologie*, Fünf Vortäge von der Generalversammlung zu Aschaffenburg, Bachem, Köln, 1913, pp. 5–17, and are further supported by Paul Allard, *Deux récentes controverses*, Revues des questions historiques 95, N.S. 51 (1914), pp. 83–101, at pp. 89–101. The same dating is maintained by Sisto Scaglia in *Il Labaro di Costantino*, La Scuola cattolica, Anno 41, serie 5, vol. 2 (1913), pp. 26–38. J. Maurice would date the introduction of the Labarum to the year 317 (? 316), when the sons of Constantine were made Caesars: cf. *Bulletin de la Société nationale des Antiquaires de France*, 1903, pp. 310–17, *ibid.*, 1904, pp. 212–20; *Comptes Rendus, Académie des Inscriptions et Belles Lettres*, 1908, pp. 156–7; *ibid.*, 1909, p. 179; *ibid.*, 1910, p. 101; *Numismatique Constantinienne*, vol. 1, pp. cv–cvii, cxxvii. The numismatic evidence for the Labarum begins only after the victory over Licinius, when Constantine had become the sole ruler of the Roman world, and at the same time that the radiate crown disappears from the coinage, cf. Otto Schönewolf, *Die Darstellung der Auferstehung Christi: ihre Entstehung ind ihre ältesten Denkmäler* (= Studien über christliche Denkmäler, ed. Johannes Ficker, Heft 9), Dieterich, Leipzig, 1909, p. 12; J. Maurice, *Numismatique Constantinienne*, vol. 2, p. 513.

On several questions modern scholars have as yet come to no decision. (i) Does Eusebius in his description of the Labarum describe the same form of the Christian monogram as Lactantius? For the negative answer, cf. e.g. P. Batiffol in *Bulletin de la Société nationale des Antiquaires de France*, 1913, pp. 211–16, at pp. 212–13; Henri Grégoire in *Byzantion* 2 (1925, published 1926), p. 408, n. 1. For the affirmative, cf. e.g. M. Sulzberger, *Le Symbole de la Croix et les Monogrammes de Jésus chez les premiers Chrétiens*, Byzantion *ibid.*, pp. 337–448, at p. 407. (ii) How should the description of the monogram as given by Lactantius be translated? The passage is one of extreme difficulty, and totally diverse interpretations of it have been given by modern scholars. In the first place it is uncertain whether the *Colbertinus*, which 'quoique assez ancien est un fort mauvais manuscript' (Sulzberger, *loc. cit.*), preserves the true reading. H. Grégoire proposes to read 'Facit ut iussus est et [I] transversa X littera, summo capite circumflexo', or 'transversa X littera [I]' etc. *Byzantion, loc. cit.*, pp. 406 n. 2, 407.[1] 'L'omission est toute naturelle, et précisément dans la

[1] For the difficulty of the absence of this iota from the text of Lactantius,

description du monogramme par Paulin de Nole la lettre I, garantie par le mètre, a sauté également: Carmen xix, v. 623. Nam rigor obstipus facit [I], quod in Hellade iota est.' On the interpretation of this passage of Paulinus of Nola, cf. J. Maurice, *Les Textes de Lactance et de Paulin de Nole relatifs au monogramme du Christ*, Bulletin de la Société nationale des Antiquaires de France, 1913, pp. 262–6. For the study of the meaning of the account of Lactantius, cf. especially P. Franchi de' Cavalieri in *Studi Romani* I (see p. 60), P. Bordeaux, *Revue des Études grecques* 26 (1913), pp. 88–91; Maurice, for references see above; add *Numismatique Constantinienne*, vol. 2, pp. l–li; Batiffol (see citation on p. 61); Sulzberger, *op. cit.*, pp. 402–8. Thus at present there is no agreement amongst scholars on the original form of the Constantinian monogram. (iii) The question of the significance of the monogram is still debated; some, as Gardthausen or Costa, would maintain its originally pagan character; Sulzberger (*op. cit.*, p. 412) has recently suggested that it may in origin have been the personal monogram of Constantius Chlorus. For my own part I can have little doubt that it was intended by Constantine from the first to bear a Christian interpretation, and the monogram is the peculiar feature of the Labarum—Eusebius, *V.C.* 2, 16 'montre bien que c'est le monogramme qui constitue le *Labarum*', Maurice, *Numismatique Constantinienne*, vol. 2, p. 512, n. 1—it is that which is the distinctive element in the Christian standard (so, I gather, Bratke, in *Das Monogramm Konstantins des Grossen*, Festschrift des Gymnasiums zu Jauer, 1892; this paper I have not been able to consult); cf. O. Schönewolf, *op. cit.* (see p. 61), p. 17, n. 1. (iv) What was the character of the statue of Constantine erected in Rome and did it bear the cross simply, or was some form of the monogram or the Labarum included (Eusebius, *H.E.* 9, 9, 10, *V.C.* 1, 40)? Eusebius in the *H.E.* says that the statue held in its right hand τοῦ σωτηρίου πάθους τὸ σωτήριον σημεῖον: the inscription attributed Constantine's victory τούτῳ σωτηριώδει σημείῳ. In the *V.C.* Eusebius speaks of a σταυρός and ὑψηλὸν δόρυ σταυροῦ σχήματι. This account of the statue given by Eusebius it is, in my judgement, difficult to question; it can no longer be treated with the scepticism of Burckhardt, cf. V. Schultze, *Untersuchungen zur Geschichte Konstantins d. Gr.*, Zeitschrift für Kirchengeschichte 7 (1885), pp. 343–52; *id.*, *Quellenuntersuchungen zur Vita Constantini des Eusebius, ibid.*, 14 (1894), pp. 510 sqq. It is strange that such a scholar as Eduard Schwartz can still write 'Nach einem zeit-

cf. Pierre Batiffol, *Bulletin de la Société nationale des Antiquaires de France*, 1913, p. 214; J. Maurice, *ibid.*, p. 216.

genössischen Festredner beschloss der Senat ihm [Constantine] eine Statue zu errichten die ihn als Gott darstellte. Die Möglichkeit, dass dies in christlicher Umdeutung an den Bischof von Cäsarea, der nie in Rom war, berichtet wurde, liegt zu nahe, als dass es geraten wäre, aus seiner Erzählung Schlüsse zu ziehen' in *Meister der Politik* (see p. 37), 1922, I, p. 192[1]; cf. Maurice, *Numismatique Constantinienne*, ii, pp. xlvi, lvi, lvii; Sulzberger, *op. cit.* (see p. 61), pp. 411–12. Some would give to this cross a neutral or a pagan character, e.g. Sulzberger, *op. cit.*, p. 412. I believe that it can only have had a Christian significance. Further I see no reason to think that τὸ σωτήριον σημεῖον in the hand of the statue was other than a simple cross,[2] and it is at least possible to see in this action of Constantine a confirmation of the story of the Vision of the Cross, though I would agree with Batiffol that in the words of Lactantius 'ut *caeleste signum dei* notaret in scutis' the adjective *caeleste* is equivalent to *sublime* or *maximum* signum—terms elsewhere used for the cross by Lactantius (see Batiffol, *op. cit.* [see p. 61], p. 215)—and does not (as has been suggested by A. Knöpfler, *Konstantins Kreuzesvision*, Historisch-politische Blätter &c. 141 (1908), pp. 193–4, by H. Schrörs, *Konstantins des Grossen Kreuzerscheinung*, Bonn, 1913, p. 14, and by F. Kampers, *Vom Werdegange der abendländischen Kaisermystik*, Teubner, Leipzig, 1924, p. 150) signify distinctly 'the cross which Constantine had seen *in the heavens*'. The Labarum is doubtless described by Eusebius as he himself saw it, i.e. at a date after the creation of the Caesars in 317, but I fail to see why Constantine should not have added to the Labarum in 317 (or after) the medallions of his sons, as Franchi de' Cavalieri suggests. I find it therefore difficult to conclude with Maurice that there cannot have existed a Labarum before 317. If the vision of the Christian monogram before the battle of the Milvian Bridge is a development from an earlier vision of the Cross, the Labarum may be regarded as a summary of Constantine's personal experience. The campaign as a whole represented the victory of the Cross—hence τὸ σωτήριον σημεῖον in the hand of the statue—but the summary expression of both visions—the Labarum—although its introduction was antedated by Eusebius,[3] may have been adopted by Constantine, it

---

[1] Cf. Duruy, *Histoire des Romains* (see p. 35), vol. 7, pp. 56–7—a pure misunderstanding on the part of Eusebius of a pagan divine symbol.

[2] I confess that I regard as very hazardous the suggestion of Wilpert that this statue is represented on Constantine's triumphal arch, cf. *Bullettino della commissione archeologica communale di Roma* 50 (1922, published 1923), at pp. 47–51.

[3] 'Euseb hat die Daten wohlbewusst verschoben. Er schreibt nach dem Tode Konstantins und will das flavische Haus glorifizieren. So projiziert er

would seem to me, as the standard of his own bodyguard (cf. J. Maurice, *Numismatique Constantinienne*, vol. 2, p. 512; Monaci suggests a *cavalry* guard, *Nuovo Bullettino di Archaeologia cristiana* 13, 1907, pp. 60–1) at any time after the victory of the Milvian Bridge. It would thus appear to me impossible precisely to date the invention of the Labarum, though it may well have taken place in A.D. 312.

A few references may be given to further literature on the subject: for a list of representations of the Labarum, cf. Grosse, article *Labarum*, in Kroll-Pauly-Wissowa, *Realencyclopädie* 12 (1924), coll. 240–2; and see G. S. Graziosi, *Frammento di sarcofago con gli emblemi del Labaro di Costantino*, Nuovo Bullettino di Archaeologia cristiana 19 (1913), pp. 131–6; A. Monaci, *La Palestina ed il Labaro e le sculture dell'Arco di Costantino, ibid.*, 13 (1907), pp. 55–61. For the various forms of the Christian monogram the most valuable study is now that of Sulzberger (see p. 61); for a useful summary of the evidence for the various forms of the Christian monogram appearing on the coinage of Constantine, cf. V. Schultze, *Die christlichen Münzprägungen unter den Konstantinern*, Zeitschrift für Kirchengeschichte 44, N.F. 7 (1925), pp. 321–37, at p. 334. For the etymology of the word Labarum, cf. H. Grégoire, *Byzantion* 4 (1927–8, published 1929), pp. 477–82: 'L'*etymon* de λάβορον doit être un terme incorrect du latin des camps: laureum (signum ou vexillum)'—it does look as though the riddle were solved at last. The Christian significance of the Labarum is perhaps best brought out by O. Schönewolf (*op. cit.*, pp. 13–16). I have not been able to consult (i) Monaci, *La visione e il labaro di Costantino*, Rome, 1913, or (ii) C. Maes, *Il primo trofeo della croce eretta da Costantino il Grande nel Foro romano*, Cuggiani, 1901, but see a summary of the author's views in *Nuovo Bullettino di Archaeologia cristiana* 19 (1913), pp. 58–9.

Finally, a word of warning may be added. It is customary to find in bibliographies on the subject (e.g. Gardthausen, Grosse) a reference to the work of J.-P. Desroches, *Le Labarum, Étude critique et archéologique*, Champion, Paris, 1894, pp. xxvii, 520. Have these scholars read the book? Its title is only chosen 'comme le symbole et le résumé du plus grand drame qui ait illustré le IVe siècle'. The work is a naive and guileless product of local patriotism claiming for Chalon-sur-Saône the honour of being the place

die Lage von 324–5 in die frühere Zeit, ins Jahr 312, zurück.' O. Schönewolf, *op. cit.*, p. 12, n. 4, and cf. *ibid.*, pp. 44–7, and p. 47 *supra*. If the Labarum were adopted not long after and as a result of the successful campaign of 312, as, in my view, may well have been the case, Eusebius may simply have made an unintentional mistake.

where Constantine was granted the divine revelation of the Cross.[1] This 'étude critique', it is true, understands the term in a peculiar sense, but how can one be angry with its author when he disarms our wrath with such engaging frankness? 'S'il y a eu témérité dans son entreprise qu'on le lui pardonne en vue de sa bonne foi (p. xix) . . . . l'enfant inconsidéré prévoit moins les précipices et il s'élance en avant, et quelquefois il arrive au but, *audaces fortuna iuvat*. Nous jouerons l'enfant de la fortune' (p. 21).

There is less excuse for the author of a lengthy study to which this book gave rise: G. Canet, *Le Labarum*, Annales de l'Académie de Macon, 2me Série, T. 12 (1895), pp. 177–241; this and the same author's article *Le Labarum*, Revue du clergé français, 4me année, T. 1 (1898), pp. 5–22 are alike, in my judgement, valueless.

It would appear to me improbable that the reader will gain much profit from the lengthy excursus on the Labarum contained in the work of F. Kampers cited in this note (see p. 63).

34. *The Battle of the Milvian Bridge.* For the bridge itself, cf. G. Tomassetti, *La Campagna romana*, Loescher, Roma, 1913, vol. 3, pp. 232–6. The reconstruction of the battle is hotly disputed; it will suffice to mention the most important modern studies: O. Seeck, *Geschichte des Untergangs*, &c., vol. 1 (2nd edn., 1897), c. 4, *Die Schlacht an der Milvischen Brücke*, especially pp. 129 sqq. and pp. 492–4 (with criticism of Moltke's view: see his *Wanderbuch*, 4th ed., Berlin, 1879, pp. 115 sqq.); A. Monaci, *La Battaglia ad 'Saxa Rubra' e il Bassorilievo Costantiniano*, Dissertazioni della Pontificia Accademia Romana di Archaeologia, Ser. 2, T. 8 (1903), Roma, pp. 105–34; F. Grossi-Gondi, *La Battaglia di Costantino Magno a 'Saxa Rubra'*, Civiltà cattolica, Ann. 63 (1912), vol. 4, pp. 385–403; *id.*, *La grande vittoria di Costantino* in *Letture Costantiniane*, Desclee, Roma, 1914, pp. 61–90; G. Costa, *La Battaglia di Costantino a Ponte Milvio*, Bilychnis 2 (1913), pp. 197–208 (with plans); criticism by G. Costa of the view of Grossi Gondi in Bilychnis 3 (1914), at p. 87; I have been unable to procure G. Biasotti, *La grande battaglia di Costantino contro Massenzio da Saxa Rubra al Pons Milvius 28 Ottobre 312*, Roma, 1912, but his view of the course of the battle is reproduced in J. Maurice, *Constantin le Grand*, Éditions Spes, Paris, n.d., pp. 41–7; A Monaci, *La campagna di Costantino in Italia nel 312*, Nuovo Bullettino di Archaeologia cristiana 19 (1913), pp. 43–69. See further K. Ritter von Landmann, *Konstantin der*

---

[1] For a similar instance of local patriotism, cf. H. Laven, *Konstantin der Grosse und das Zeichen am Himmel*, Lintz, Trier, 1902; the worthy Pfarrer in Leiwen a/Mosel locates the Vision of the Cross on the 'Kron', a hill between Neumagen and Leiwen, pp. 28–30.

Grosse als Feldherr in Konstantin der Grosse und seine Zeit (see p. 51), pp. 143–54 at pp. 147 sqq. For Constantine as the new Moses after the destruction of Maxentius in the waters of the Tiber, cf. E. Becker, *Konstantin der Grosse, der 'neue Moses'. Die Schlacht am Pons Milvius und die Katastrophe am Schilfmeer*, Zeitschrift für Kirchengeschichte 31 (1910), pp. 161–71; *id.*, *Protest gegen den Kaiserkult und Verherrlichung des Sieges am Pons Milvius in der christlichen Kunst der konstantinischen Zeit* in Konstantin der Grosse und seine Zeit (see p. 51), pp. 155–90; and cf. J. Maurice, *Comptes Rendus: Académie des Inscriptions et Belles Lettres*, Paris, 1919, at pp. 283–6. For the interesting question raised by the sarcophagi discussed by Becker [cf. N. H. Baynes, *History*, 14 (1930), p. 297] see now Jean Lassus, *Quelques représentations du 'Passage de la Mer Rouge' dans l'art chrétien d'Orient et d'Occident*, Mélanges d'Archéologie et d'Histoire 46 (1929), pp. 159–81 with 2 fig.—a valuable study, and for Gaul as an art centre, cf. O. Schönewolf, *op. cit.* (see p. 61), pp. 36–40.

It is important to remember that Constantine's march into Italy is *not* a crusade against a persecutor of the Christians; though Maxentius was a pagan fostering ancient pagan traditions, he had none of the anti-Christian fervour of his eastern colleague Maximin. 'Maxence c'était l'empire s'ancrant de plus en plus dans sa tradition païenne; Constantin c'était l'empire décidément favorable au christianisme et ouvert à son influence.' Cf. L. Duchesne, *Constantin et Maxence*, Nuovo Bullettino di Archeologia cristiana 19 (1913), pp. 29–35, at p. 34.

35. It is unnecessary for the purpose of this lecture to attempt any bibliography of the extensive recent literature in which the Arch of Constantine has been discussed; it will suffice to refer to S. B. Platner and T. Ashby, *A Topographical Dictionary of Ancient Rome*, Oxford University Press, London, Milford, 1929, pp. 36–8, and to note that the famous articles of De Rossi, which in 1863 established that the traditional form of the inscription upon the arch was not due to any later alteration of the original text, have been reprinted in *Nuovo Bullettino di Archeologia cristiana* 19 (1913), pp. 7–19 and 21–8. For admirable reproductions of the Constantinian sculptures of the arch see the plates accompanying the article of J. Wilpert on *Le Sculture del fregio dell'arco trionfale di Costantino*, Bullettino della commissione archeologica comunale di Roma 50 (1922, published 1923), pp. 13–57.

36. *Instinctu divinitatis.* The remarks in the text are directed against the view of G. Costa who contends that the words 'instinctu

divinitatis, mentis magnitudine' are parallel phrases: the 'divinitas' is Constantine himself. This view was expressed in an article in the *Rassegna contemporanea* (out of print, see p. 37), and defended in *Critica e Tradizione: osservazioni sulla politica e sulla religione di Costantino*, Bilychnis 3 (1914), pp. 85–105 at pp. 96–8. He would translate ' "Spinto dal suo proprio nume e indotto dalle sue grandi vedute Costantino ha vinto il nemico" egli cioè ha voluto e saputo vincere; per l'appunto questo sostengono i panegiristi', p. 96. *Suae* is not placed after *mentis*, it is therefore not needed after *divinitatis*; the form of the whole phrase is chiastic, so that we must expect not 'opposizione di concetti', but 'contrapposizione delle qualità'. He refers in support of his view to Pan. 9 (now in Teubner edition of 1911, Pan. 12), cc. 4 and 5, 13, and 22, and very probably 2, 3, and 11. He boldly states 'non si può concepire la divinità suprema distinta dall' imperatore'. I think that Costa has failed to follow the argument of the panegyrist which is surely this: this incredible victory is a superhuman achievement; what God aided Constantine we do not know (Quisnam te deus, &c., 9, 2), that is Constantine's secret. 'Habes profecto aliquod cum illa mente divina, Constantine, secretum quae delegata nostri diis minoribus cura uni se tibi dignatur ostendere. Alioquin fortissime, sic quoque, cum viceris, redde rationem' (9, c. 2). 'Dic quaeso quid in consilio nisi divinum numen habuisti?' (9, 4). Or is it enough to say that, since the better cause must triumph, you were led merely by your own *ratio*—'sua enim cuique prudentia deus est'—and by the justice of your arms? Were these the gods? Was the divine counsel your own? Surely the argument of the whole speech is destroyed if we accept this second alternative as the view of the panegyrist (cf. H. Schrörs, *Konstantins des Grossen Kreuzerscheinung*, Hanstein, Bonn, 1913, c. 1): his contention is 'non dubiam te, sed promissam divinitus petere victoriam' (c. 3); 'ipsi etiam qui tibi in consilio erant, ipse etiam praefectus haerere cum tu divino monitus instinctu' saved the lives of the defeated (c. 11); the 'divina mens et ipsius urbis aeterna maiestas' drove Maxentius from the shelter of the walls of Rome (c. 16); the speech closes with a prayer to the Unknown God—'quem enim te ipse dici velis, scire non possumus' (cf. c. 2, 'quisnam te deus quae tam praesens hortata est maiestas', &c.)—to save the emperor. With this we should contrast 'statim bellum auspicatus a Tiberi ad Rhenum, immo (ut omen et similitudo nominis [sit] et tua, imperator, magnitudo animi pollicetur) a Tusco Albula ad Germanicum Albam prolaturus imperium' (c. 21). 'Divino monitus instinctu'—'Heaven's part—'magnitudine animi'—Constantine's contribution to his victories: so the Panegyrist. 'Instinctu divinitatis, mentis magnitudine': thus the inscription on the Arch. I cannot but feel that the meaning is the same. I desire to guard against any misapprehension: I agree completely with Wilpert's statement that 'la famosa frase *instinctu divinitatis* non ha niente di cristiano, essa è tolta dalla terminologia di culti idolatrici'. *Bullettino della commissione archeologica comunale di Roma* 50 (1922, published 1923), p. 17; cf. J. Maurice, *Numismatique Constantinienne*, vol. 2, p. cxiv. But the expression may be regarded as evidence that pagans in Rome knew of Constantine's belief that his victory had been the result of divine intervention.

37. Cf. N. H. Baynes, *Two Notes on the Great Persecution*. (ii) *The Chronology of the ninth book of the Historia Ecclesiastica of Eusebius*, Classical Quarterly 18 (1924), at pp. 193–4; H. J. Lawlor (Reply), and N. H. Baynes and G. W. Richardson (Rejoinder), *ibid.* 19 (1925), 94–100. Dr. Lawlor still maintains his own view of Eusebian chronology in *Eusebius Bishop of Caesarea. The Ecclesiastical History and the Martyrs of Palestine translated with introduction and notes by H. J. L. and J. E. L. Oulton*, S.P.C.K., London, 2 vols., 1927 and 1928, vol. ii, pp. 37–40, but this defence does not convince me. Thus Dr. Lawlor writes (p. 38) that Eusebius 'informs us that the toleration edict of April 311 was issued *in the eighth year*' of the persecution; I find it difficult to give this translation to the words (τοῦ διωγμοῦ) λωφᾶν γε μὴν μετ᾽ ὄγδοον ἔτος ἐναρξαμένου H.E. 8, 16, 1. For Constantine as senior Augustus, cf. Lactantius, *De mort. pers.* 44, 11, and see J. Maurice, *La véracité historique de Lactance*, Comptes Rendus, Académie des Inscriptions et Belles Lettres, 1908, pp. 146–59, at p. 158, and *Numismatique Constantinienne*, Leroux, Paris, 1911, vol. ii, p. 240.

38. For a convenient collection of the documents relating to the early history of Donatism, cf. Hans von Soden, *Urkunden zur Entstehungsgeschichte des Donatismus* (= Hans Lietzmann's Kleine Texte für Vorlesungen und Übungen, No. 122), Weber, Bonn, 1913. Letter to Anullinus, Eusebius, *H.E.*, 10, 5, 15–17.

39. Eusebius, *H.E.*, 10, 6, 1–5.

40. Monsignor Batiffol has failed to bring out the full significance of the letter in his comments published in *Bulletin d'ancienne littérature et d'archéologie chrétiennes* 3 (1913), pp. 259–60. In respect of the chronology of these documents Seeck's *Regesten* must be corrected; the report of Anullinus of 15 April 313 [Augustine ep. 88, 2 and Coll. Carth. iii. 216–20; von Soden adds other references, *op. cit.* (see note 38) p. 12, n.] is a reply to the letter reproduced in

Eusebius, *H.E.* 10, 7, and not to that reproduced in Eusebius, *H.E.* 10, 5, 15. This can be seen from a comparison of the two texts:

διόπερ ἐκείνους τοὺς εἴσω τῆς σοι πεπιστευμένης ἐν τῇ καθολικῇ ἐκκλησίᾳ, ᾗ Καικιλιανὸς ἐφέστηκε, τὴν ἐξ αὐτῶν ὑπηρεσίαν τῇ ἁγίᾳ ταύτῃ θρηκσείᾳ παρέχοντας, οὕσπερ κληρικοὺς ἐπονομάζειν εἰώθασιν, ἀπὸ πάντων ἅπαξ ἁπλῶς τῶν λειτουργιῶν βούλομαι ἀλειτουργήτους διαφυλαχθῆναι κ.τ.λ.

with 'Scripta caelestia maiestatis vestrae accepta atque adorata Caeciliano et his, qui sub eodem agunt quique clerici appellantur devotio mea apud acta parvitatis meae insinuare curavit eosdemque hortata est, ut unitate consensu omnium facta, cum omni omnino munere indulgentia[e] maiestatis vestrae liberati esse videantur, catholicae custodita sanctitate legis debita reverentia ac divinis rebus inserviant'. There is therefore no reason to place the letter to Anullinus reproduced in Eusebius, *H.E.* 10, 5, 15 or the letter to Caecilian (*H.E.* 10, 6) in March 313 (Seeck, *Regesten*, p. 160); I would date them to the winter of 312. Further, the letter to Anullinus reported in *H.E.* 10, 7 must be removed from 31 October 313 (Seeck, *ibid.*, p. 161); it must have reached Africa and been published there some days before 15 April. This does not, of course, exclude the possibility that the letter was written by Constantine at some date *before* the meeting at Milan.

41. On the account given by Lactantius of this meeting, cf. N. H. Baynes, *Journal of Roman Studies* 18 (1928), p. 228.

42. The Edicts of toleration issued during the years 311–13 must be considered in relation to each other, if one would understand aright the significance of Constantine's action. The more important recent studies (in which reference to the earlier literature on the subject will be found) are the following: Th. Keim, *Die römischen Toleranzedikte für das Christenthum (311–313) und ihr geschichtlicher Werth* in Theologische Jahrbücher 11 (1852), 207–59; Belser, *Grammatisch-kritische Erklärung von Laktantius de mortibus persecutorum cap. 34: Toleranzedikt des Galerius*, Festprogramm des Königlichen Gymnasiums in Ellwangen, 1889; Hermann Hülle, *Die Toleranzerlasse römischer Kaiser für das Christentum bis zum Jahre 313*, Dissertation of Greifswald, Berlin, 1895; Karl Bihlmeyer, *Das Toleranzedikt des Galerius von 311*, &c., Theologische Quartalschrift 94 (1912), pp. 411–27, 527–89; id. *Das angebliche Toleranzedikt Konstantins von 312. Mit Beiträgen zur Mailänder Konstitution (313)*, ibid., 96 (1914), pp. 65–100, 198–224; Valerian Şesan, *Kirche und Staat*, &c. (see p. 37), Czernowitz, 1911; Emilio Galli, *L'editto di Milano del 313*, La Scuola Cattolica, Anno XLI (1913), Serie vᵃ, vol. 2, 39–73 (there are other articles on the

Edict of Milan in this centenary fascicule May–June 1913);
Joseph Wittig, *Das Toleranzreskript von Mailand 313* in Konstantin
der Grosse und seine Zeit (see p. 51), 1913, pp. 40–65; P. Batiffol,
Les étapes de la conversion de Constantin, II. *L'Édit de Milan*, in Bulletin d'ancienne littérature et d'archéologie chrétiennes 3 (1913),
pp. 241–64; J. Maurice, *Note sur le préambule placé par Eusèbe en tête
de l'Édit de Milan, ibid.*, 4 (19**14**), 45–7 (cf. *id., Critique des textes
d'Eusèbe et de Lactance relatifs à l'Édit de Milan*, Bulletin de la Société
nationale des Antiquaires de France, 1913, pp. 349–54 = practically the same article); F. Martroye, *A propos de 'l'édit de Milan', ibid.*,
4 (1914), 47–52; P. Batiffol, *Le seizième centenaire de l'édit de Milan:
L'édit de Milan et les origines de la liberté religieuse*, Le Correspondant
for 10 March 1913, and *La Paix Constantinienne et le Catholicisme*,
Lecoffre, Paris, 1914, pp. 203–67; R. Pichon, *La liberté de con-
science dans l'ancienne Rome: à propos du seizième anniversaire de l'Édit de
Milan*, Revue des Deux Mondes, Année 83, Période 6, T. 16 (1913),
pp. 314–48 (an admirable essay); J. Schrijnen, *Konstantijn de Groote
en het edikt van Milaan*, Van Rossum, Utrecht, 1913; Filippo Meda,
Costantino e l'editto di Milano, Rassegna Nazionale, Ann. 35, vol.
189 (1913), pp. 473–88 (an interesting study); A. Brilliantov,
Imperator Konstantin Velikii i milanskii edikt 313 goda, Petrograd, 1916;
J. R. Knipfing, *Das angebliche 'Mailänder Edikt' v. J. 313 im Lichte
der neueren Forschung*, Zeitschrift für Kirchengeschichte 40, N.F. 3
(1922), pp. 206–18, *id., The Edict of Galerius (311 A.D.) reconsidered*,
Revue belge de Philologie et d'Histoire 1 (1922), pp. 693–705, and
a synthesis of both papers in *Religious Tolerance during the early part
of the reign of Constantine the Great 306–313*, in The Catholic Historical
Review N.S. 4 (1925), pp. 483–503; R. Laqueur, *Die beiden Fas-
sungen des sog. Toleranzedikts von Mailand* in 'Επιτύμβιον Heinrich
Swoboda dargebracht, Gebrüder Stiepel, Reichenberg, 1927,
pp.132–41; Hildegard Florin,*Untersuchungen zur diocletianischen Christenverfolgung*, Dissertation, Giessen, 1928. Marcel Viller's article *La
Paix de l'Église. L'édit de l'année 313*, in Études (Paris), T. 135, 50ᵉ
Année (1913), pp. 438–64, kindly lent to me by Father Thurston,
is an unimportant narrative covering the period 303–23; it lays
stress upon the tact and caution of Constantine's religious policy.
For a comparison and discussion of the Lactantian and Eusebian
texts, cf. I. A. Heikel, *De Constantini imperatoris scriptis edendis*, Inbjudning-Skrift of the University of Helsingfors, dated 29 March
1916, pp. 17–28. It is unnecessary to enumerate here the general
histories containing a consideration of the toleration edicts such
as e.g. those of Manaresi, Linsenmayr and Karl Müller.

On the question whether or no there was in fact an Edict of

Milan, cf. O. Seeck, *Das sogenannte Edikt von Mailand*, in Zeitschrift für Kirchengeschichte 12 (1891), pp. 381–6; the reply of F. Görres, *Eine Bestreitung des Edicts von Mailand durch O. Seeck* in Zeitschrift für wissenschaftliche Theologie 35 (1892), pp. 282–95 is quite ineffective. Later writers have at least admitted that the word 'Edict', if used in its precise meaning, must be abandoned, though the existence of a 'constitution' of Milan is generally maintained, cf. A. Crivellucci, *L'editto di Milano*, Studi Storici 1 (1892), pp. 239–50; *id.*, *Intorno all'editto di Milano, ibid.*, 4 (1895), pp. 267–73; we must add to Seeck's denials 'che tuttavia un editto o un manifesto di Milan dal quale direttamente dipendessero il rescritto di Nicomedia *quam feliciter* e l'editto di Massimino κατὰ πάντα τρόπον quantumque non ci sia pervenuto testualmente, dovette necessariamente esistere' (p. 272).

For the legal questions and the effect of the edict upon rights of property, cf. C. Carassai, *La politica religiosa di Costantino il Grande e la proprietà della chiesa*, Archivio della Reale Società Romana di Storia patria 24 (1901), pp. 95–157; G. Schnyder, *L'editto di Milano ed i recenti studi critici che lo riguardano*, Dissertazioni della Pontificia Accad. Romana di Archeologia, Ser. ii, T. 8 (1903), Roma, pp. 149–79; C. A. Santucci, *L'editto di Milano specialmente nei riguardi giuridichi*, Rivista internazionale di scienze sociali e discipline ausiliarie for 31 March 1913; this is inaccessible to me, but it appears that the views expressed in this article are presented in a revised form in *Nuovo Bullettino di Archeologia cristiana* 19 (1913), pp. 71–5; for criticism see G. L. Perugi, *La fonte giuridica dell' editto di Milano* (an article based upon De Rossi's theory of *collegia funeraticia*), Roma e l'Oriente 3 (Nov.–Dec. 1913), pp. 13–40 (273–300); Émile Chénon, *Les conséquences juridiques de l'édit de Milan (313)*, Nouvelle Revue historique de droit, français et étranger 38 (1914), pp. 255–63; cf. J. P. Kirsch: *Die christlichen Cultusgebäude in der vorkonstantinischen Zeit* in Festschrift zum elfhundertjährigen Jubiläum des Deutschen Campo Santo in Rom, Hrg. v Dr. Stephan Ehses, Freiburg, 1897, pp. 6–21. The real difficulty in estimating the effects produced by the policy of Constantine lies in the fact that scholars have not yet satisfactorily explained by what (if any) legal title the property of the Christian Church was held in the period before the outbreak of the last great persecution; there would seem to be no evidence in support of De Rossi's theory that the early Christians formed *collegia* which were recognized by the Roman state (cf. G. B. de Rossi, *La Roma sotterranea cristiana*, Cromo-litografia Pontificia, Rome, 1864, vol. 1, pp. 101–8); for the criticism of this theory, cf. Waltzing, *Les*

corporations de l'ancienne Rome et la charité, Compte rendu du troi-
sième Congrès scientifique international des Catholiques tenu à
Bruxelles du 3 au 8 septembre 1894, 5me Section, Sciences Historiques, Société belge de Librairie, Bruxelles 1895, pp. 165–90,
cf. *ibid.*, p. 488; *id.*, *La Thèse de J. B. de Rossi sur les collèges funéraires
chrétiens*, Bulletin de la Classe des Lettres et des Sciences morales
et politiques et de la Classe des Beaux Arts, Académie royale de
Belgique, 1912, No. 6(Bruxelles), pp. 387–401; *id.*, article *Collegia*
in *Dictionnaire d'archéologie chrétienne*, T. 3, 2me Partie, 1914, coll.
2107–2140; L. Duchesne, *Les origines chrétiennes* [lithographed
lectures], nouvelle édition (1st edn. ? 1878–81), 2me Partie, n.d.,
pp. 393–403 (The British Museum Catalogue suggests 1891); *id.*,
Histoire ancienne de l'Église, vol. 1, 4me édition, Fontemoing, Paris,
1908, pp. 381–7; Brilliantov, *op. cit.* (see p. 40), pp. 127–31, who
refers to I. Berdnikov, *Gosudarstvennoe polozhenie religii v rimsko-
vizantiiskoi imperii*, vol. 1, Kazan, 1881, pp. 548–51 (the theory is
not supported by facts). Maurice Besnier, *Les catacombs de Rome*,
Leroux, Paris, 1909, cc. 2, pp. 28–47, has attempted to defend
De Rossi's theory by suggesting that in the cities of the Empire
each separate Christian parish formed a *collegium*. See further
Raymond Saleilles, *L'organisation juridique des premières communautés
chrétiennes* in Mélanges P. F. Girard, Rousseau, Paris, 1912, vol. 2,
pp. 469–509; and cf. Ed. Meynial, *Les travaux de R. Saleilles sur le
Droit romain*, in L'œuvre juridique de Raymond Saleilles, Rousseau, Paris, 1914, pp. 185–240 at pp. 218–22. It is not easy to find
any other basis for a legal claim to hold property; see the discussion of the problem in Melchiorre Roberti, *Le associazioni fune-
rarie cristiane e la proprietà ecclesiastica nei primi tre secoli*, in Studi
dedicati alla memoria di Pier Paolo Zanzucchi, &c. (= Pubblica-
zioni della Università cattolica del Sacro Cuore, Serie settima,
Scienze guiridiche, vol. 14), Società editrice Vita e Pensiero,
Milano, n.d., pp. 89–113.

It will be sufficient for my present purpose very briefly to state
my own view of the so-called 'Edict of Milan'. I believe that
Carassai (whose work has been curiously neglected by scholars)
first suggested the true method of approach to the solution of the
problem. He sought to reconstruct the original text of the Edict
by omitting from the versions given by Lactantius and Eusebius
the 'epistolatory explanations' which follow the brief enacting
clauses which preserve the natural style of an edict (Carassai, pp.
102–3). In this attempt to restore the original Edict he has been
followed by Batiffol (in *Le Correspondant*), Wittig and Galli, but
Martroye, as it seems to me, drew the natural conclusion from

those differences in style to which Carassai called attention. The text of the document which was published by Licinius in the provinces which had formerly belonged to Maximin is composed of a collection of letters written to provincial governors and therefore explaining carefully the significance of the imperial provisions. In a word, the document, as we possess it, represents letters of Constantine previously sent by him to his governors, of the same character as those preserved in the case of Roman Africa. The text thus represents, as Schnyder rightly suggested, an agreed protocol which it was intended should be issued by Licinius on his return to the East in the name of all three colleagues; that is why the meeting of Constantine and Licinius is reported by Lactantius without reference to an 'Edict of Milan'. But what is the meaning of the 'amotis omnibus conditionibus' clause in Lactantius and of the preamble which appears in the Eusebian version but is absent from the *De Mortibus*? For Maurice's view that the Eusebian version represents the original *Litterae Constantini* which Licinius abbreviated in his publication of the document in Nicomedia I have never been able to find any cogent argument. It is now customary both among Russian (e.g. Brilliantov) and West European scholars to refer these 'conditiones' to the documents published by order of Maximin. I do not find it easy to accept this explanation; it would surely be very strange if after the flight of Maximin and the 'damnatio memoriae' of the tyrant (cf. G. Zedler, *De Memoriae Damnatione quae dicitur*, Leipzig dissertation, Winter, Darmstadt, 1885, pp. 37–8, 40; cf. Eusebius, *H.E.*, 9. 11) with the consequent nullification of all his decrees, Licinius should have allowed Constantine and himself to appear in a public proclamation as responsible for those decrees. I prefer to adopt the view of Zahn, *Skizzen aus dem Leben der Alten Kirche*, 2nd ed., Deichert, Erlangen and Leipzig, 1898, pp. 376–7, which has recently been admirably championed by Bihlmeyer, and to refer these 'conditiones' to the letters of instructions sent out to his officials by Galerius at the time of the issue of his Edict of toleration in 311. It has been suggested that, though such letters of instructions are contemplated in the text of his Edict, there is no evidence that they were actually issued. But surely so startling a change in imperial policy necessarily demanded a contemporaneous dispatch of instructions to executive officers explaining the range and application of the measure. The general terms of the Edict of Galerius would in especial demand such explication. And for the Edict of 311 Constantine shared responsibility with Galerius; up to the year 309 Constantine on his coinage had not recognized any of his eastern colleagues, neither Galerius nor Severus nor Maximin, since both Severus and Maximin owed their title to Galerius. But in the month of May 309 Constantine issued coinage in the names of Maximin and Licinius: 'C'est que ce fut seulement lorsque le titre d'Auguste lui eut été attribué à lui-même par Galère qu'il reconnut l'autorité de cet empereur et se rapprocha des empereurs d'Orient, dont il fit alors frapper les monnaies'. J. Maurice, *Bulletin de la Société nationale des Antiquaires de France*, 1900, pp. 314–17, at p. 317. I am therefore inclined to think that the original protocol which Licinius carried with him from Milan to the East contained the reference to the 'conditiones' of Galerius in the form preserved by Lactantius. But as Licinius advanced into Syria and the provinces which had from the first been governed by Maximin he found considerable suspicion of these protestations of toleration; the Christians knew how such protestations had been interpreted by Maximin (cf. Laqueur's paper). Licinius therefore made more explicit reference to the earlier Edict in the form in which Eusebius presents the *Litterae Licinii*; the Eusebian preamble is thus an addition to the protocol agreed upon at Milan. If the emendation of the Eusebian text proposed by Heikel were adopted, it would reinforce this interpretation of the preamble; he would read ἀλλ' ἐπειδὴ πολλαὶ καὶ διάφοροι αἱρέσεις ἐν ἐκείνῃ τῇ ἀντι-γράφῃ, ἐν ᾗ τοῖς αὐτοῖς συνεχωρήθη ἡ τοιαύτη ἐξουσία, ἐδοκοῦν προσ-τεθεῖσθαι ἀσαφῶς κ.τ.λ., *De Constantini imperatoris scriptis edendis* (see p. 70), p. 19. It would appear to me that this is the simplest explanation of the two versions of the *Litterae Licinii*.

I should agree with Seeck that there never was an Edict of Milan: Constantine had previously to that meeting in letters to his officials anticipated the protocol of Milan which was itself composed on the basis of those letters.

43. Optatus, 1, 22.

44. Eusebius, *H.E.*, 10, 5, 18–20. I do not consider it necessary to emend the text with Seeck and substitute for Marcus the name of Merocles of Milan, cf. Seeck in *Zeitschrift für Kirchengeschichte* 10 (1889), p. 512 f. See N. H. Baynes, *Journal of Theological Studies* 26 (1925), pp. 404–5.

45. This fact was first pointed out by H. M. Gwatkin in the *Cambridge Medieval History* (1911), vol. 1, p. 12. The significance of the change has recently been brought into prominence by Erich Caspar, in his *Kleinere Beiträge zur älteren Paptsgeschichte*, Zeitschrift für Kirchengeschichte 46 (N.F. 9, 1927), pp. 341–6; in his lecture delivered at Oslo in 1928—*Historische Probleme der älteren*

Papstgeschichte, Historische Zeitschrift 139 (1929), pp. 229–41, at pp. 232–4, and (since my lecture was delivered) in his *Geschichte des Papsttums*, vol. 1, Mohr, Tübingen, 1930, pp. 109–17, 582.

46. I regard all the documents contained in the 'dossier' of Optatus as genuine. In 1889 Seeck subjected these documents to a lengthy analysis and concluded that many of them were forgeries (O. Seeck, *Quellen und Urkunden über die Anfänge des Donatismus*, Zeitschrift für Kirchengeschichte 10, pp. 505–68); in 1890 Duchesne brilliantly defended their authenticity in his masterly paper *Le Dossier du Donatisme*, Mélanges d'Archéologie et d'Histoire publiés par l'École française de Rome 10, pp. 589–650. In 1909 Seeck published a fresh study on the subject in *Urkundenfälschungen des 4. Jahrhunderts. 1. Das Urkundenbuch des Optatus*, Zeitschrift für Kirchengeschichte 30, pp. 181–227 in which he contended that the original petition of the Donatists to Constantine was a forgery, as was the letter of Constantine to Aelafius, and further that the mission of the bishops Eunomius and Olympius was an invention, and their *sententia* a fabrication. Later Batiffol maintained, *Bulletin d'ancienne littérature et d'archéologie Chrétiennes* 4 (1914), pp. 284–7, that the letters of Constantine to Aelafius and to the Council of Arles are both the work of the same forger, and that the greater part of the letter of Constantine to the Numidian bishops (A.D. 330) is also a forgery (cf. his book *La Paix constantinienne*, pp. 305–6). But to-day most students are agreed that the documents are genuine, though the difficulties of text and interpretation in large measure still await a satisfactory interpretation: cf. Heinrich Schrörs, *Drei Aktenstücke in betreff des Konzils von Arles. Textverbesserungen und Erläuterungen*, Zeitschrift der Savigny-Stiftung für Rechtsgeschichte 42, Kanonistische Abteilung 11 (Weimar) 1921, pp. 429–39; N. H. Baynes, *Optatus*, Journal of Theological Studies 26 (1924), pp. 37–44 (I have been dealt with very faithfully by my critics—'völlig undiskutierbar' . . . ; 'nicht besser steht es mit' . . . (Caspar)—and not much of this article has withstood their assaults); *id.*, *Optatus: an Addendum, ibid.*, 26 (1925), pp. 404–6; H. Stuart Jones, *Urbis Romae episcopi, ibid.*, pp. 406–7; C. H. Turner, *Adversaria Critica: Notes on the Anti-Donatist dossier and on Optatus, Books I, II, ibid.*, 27 (1926), pp. 283–96; K. Müller, *Kleine Beiträge zur alten Kirchengeschichte*, No. 12. *Zu dem Erlass Konstantins an 'Aelafius' in den Anfängen des donatistischen Streits*, Zeitschrift für die neutestamentliche Wissenschaft, &c. 24 (1925), pp. 287–90; Erich Caspar, *Kleine Beiträge zur älteren Papstgeschichte. 2 Die römische Synode von 313*, Zeitschrift für Kirchengeschichte 46, N.F. 9 (1927), pp. 333–46, and (published since my lecture)

Geschichte des Papsttums (see p. 75), pp. 582–3; cf. in general Monceaux, *Histoire littéraire de l'Afrique chrétienne*, vol. 5, Paris, 1920.

On these documents I may be allowed to make a few remarks. I still think it unnecessary to emend the name Aelafius into Ablabius: Aelafius may well have held the position of a 'vices agens praefectorum praetorio'. I am inclined to transpose the much discussed words (in the letter to Aelafius) 'sed et septem eiusdem communionis' in accordance with the bold suggestion of C. H. Turner who would read 'Ut ad Urbem Roman tam Caecilianus Carthaginiensis episcopus contra quem vel maxime diversi (for universi) saepe me convenerant, sed et septem eiusdem communionis quam etiam aliqui ex his qui ei quaedam obicienda crediderant, praesentiam sui exhiberent'. For the construction, cf. the later passage in the same letter 'tam Caecilianum', &c., 'sed et de Byzacenae . . . sed etiam aliquos', &c., and see Caspar, *Zeitschrift für Kirchengeschichte* 46, p. 340. This transposition is, it must be admitted, a violent measure, but inasmuch as the eleventh-century Paris MS. to which alone we owe the 'dossier du Donatisme' was, it would seem, copied from a very much older MS. which was in parts already mutilated and illegible, there is greater excuse for courageous treatment of the text. There is a further passage in the letter which in my judgement is in its present form hopelessly confused and demands for its understanding treatment hardly less radical. It is curious that no critic of the letter would seem to have remarked the extent of the difficulty. The passage reads: 'quare cum haec tot et tanta nimium obnixe dissensiones protrahere perviderem (sc. Constantine), ita ut nullo modo finis isdem dari posse videatur nisi et Caecilianus idem ⟨et⟩ ex his qui contra eum dissident tres aliqui in iudicium eorum qui contra Caecilianum sentiunt[1] consensumque debent,[2] ad Arelatense oppidum venire[3] iniungendum solertiae tuae duxi ut mox has litteras meas acciperes,[4] tam Caecilianum supra dictum cum aliquibus ex his, quos ipse delegerit—sed et de Byzacenae, Tripolitanae, Numidiarum et Mauretaniarum [et] provinciis singulis[5] quique[6] aliquantos ex suis perducere debebunt, quos ipsi putaverint eligendos—sed etiam aliquos ex his qui contra eundem Caecilianum dissentiunt, data evectione publica per Africam et Mauritaniam inde ad

---

[1] 'Read perhaps indicium for iudicium and quae for qui. And in the next line for consensumque debent, which I find untranslateable, the best I can suggest is consensum dederint.' C. H. Turner, *Journal of Theological Studies* 27, p. 287.   [2] Habent, Heikel.   [3] Venerint? Venirent? von Soden.

[4] ⟨cum⟩ . . . acceperis, Heikel.   [5] Singuli? von Soden.

[6] Quique aliquos, Heikel.

Hispanias brevi tractu facias navigare', &c. The part of the sentence which puzzles me is thus translated by Vassall-Phillips:[1] 'Wherefore since I perceived that these numerous and important affairs were being pertinaciously delayed by discussions, so that it appeared that no end could be made of them without both Caecilian and three of those who are making a schism against him coming to the town of Arles for the judgement of those who are opposed to Caecilian and are bound to accept him as bishop . . .' But this is simply to prejudge the issue: Constantine could not have written nonsense like this. Why should Caecilian come alone and his opponents be allowed three representatives? The rest of the sentence shows that he was to bring more supporters than three—note the list of provinces—while the Donatists can hardly have been granted a lesser number; *tres* is I think clearly corrupt. 'Qui consensum debent' is in its present position absurd. The sense demands some such re-writing of the sentence as, 'Nisi et Caecilianus idem et aliqui ex his qui ei consensum debent sed etiam aliqui eorum qui contra Caecilianum sentiunt et contra eum dissident in iudicium ad Arelatense oppidum venirent iniungendum solertiae tuae duxi . . .' I do not pretend to suggest that this wording was that of Constantine's original letter, but that some such form of transposition of the text is needed I feel certain if we are able to restore common sense to the emperor's epistle. Should it be admitted that this argument is just, it might strengthen the case for the transposition of the words 'sed et septem', &c., proposed by Dr. Turner.

In criticism of my attempt to defend the MS. reading 'remeasse prohiberent' in this letter (*Journal of Theol. Studies* 26, p. 42; *ibid.*, 26, pp. 405–6) Dr. Turner writes (*ibid.*, 27, p. 286): '*Prohiberent* is rightly objected to by von Soden, for it is quite out of the question to suppose that bishops at that day claimed or exercised secular jurisdiction: and the correction to prohiberem (which is as old as Dupin's edition) is, I think, clearly right.' I fear that I am inpenitent: would the bishops have regarded their decision as an exercise of *secular* jurisdiction? They had declared against the Donatists; they were met to secure the peace of the African church; how could that peace be maintained if the leaders of the Donatist faction were allowed to return to the province which they had thrown into confusion? As an assembly of bishops purporting to exercise in good faith an ecclesiastical discipline they could surely order their refractory colleagues to absent themselves from Africa.

[1] O. R. Vassall-Phillips, *The Work of St. Optatus, Bishop of Milevis, against the Donatists*, &c. Longmans, Green & Co., London, 1917, pp. 385–6.

There is a precise parallel for such action only a few years later at the Council of Tyre when the bishops condemning Athanasius ψηφίζονται αὐτὸν μηκέτι τὴν Ἀλεξάνδρειαν οἰκεῖν, ἵνα μή, φησὶ, θορύβους καὶ στάσεις παρὼν ἐργάζηται (Sozomen, H.E. 2, 25). I now desire to withdraw my proposed emendation of the text (*Journal of Theological Studies* 26, p. 405). In fourth-century Latin *ipse* is, I think, used for *is* when reference is made to persons or things previously mentioned; so e.g. in the letter of the Council of Arles to Pope Silvester 'in quibus et apostoli cotidie sedent et cruor ipsorum . . . dei gloriam testatur'. The usage is frequent in the constitutions of the *C. Th.*, cf. e.g. ii. 10, 6, 4; ii. 17, 1, 15; iii. 31, 1, 2; iv. 22, 1, 13; v. 1, 1, 1^2; vi. 8, 1, 6; 8, 1, 9; 12, 1, 5; 23, 1, 7; 24, 9, 8; 26, 14, 17, &c. I would therefore retain the MS. reading 'ipsos remeasse prohiberent'. The interest of the point lies in the fact that, if this reading can be upheld, it will have been the bishops who suggested to Constantine his own subsequent action in endeavouring to retain the leaders of both parties in Italy.

In answer to a criticism of my paper made by Dr. Dölger, *Byzantinische Zeitschrift* 26 (1926), p. 188, I would suggest that Constantine directed the bishops to travel by way of Spain not merely in order to avoid the concentration of the hostile parties in Carthage, but also to prevent the creation of a danger-centre in Rome. The later history of the Donatist controversy proves that this was no idle fear. I still think that the 'brevi tractu' of the letter to Aelafius is like the 'more healthy climate' of Nicaea a diplomatic subterfuge veiling imperial policy.

I withdraw my own remarks on the reading 'Urbis Romae episcopi' in favour of Dr. Turner's explanation.

Since it is not necessary for my present purpose to discuss the letter of the bishops assembled at Arles to Pope Silvester I may add here that in view of Dr. Turner's challenge 'I think I could defy any one to produce a fourth-century example of the use of dioecesis in any vernacular document in an ecclesiastical connexion', I should now take dioecesis in its civil sense. Being unwilling to to reject the lectio difficilior *diocheseos*—a Greek genitive in a Latin document—I would read with Koch 'qui maiores dioceseos partes tenes' [see *Zeitschrift für Kirchengeschichte* 44 (1925), p. 183]. This, I would suggest, is simply a periphrasis for Rome as the capital of Italy, 'partes illae "in quibus et apostoli cotidie sedent et cruor ipsorum sine intermissione dei gloriam testatur"', as it has been described earlier in the letter.

47. This use of *noster* by the emperor at this date is very significant; it should be contrasted with the 'et consuetudinis *vestrae*

celebrate solemnia' of *C. Th.* 9, 16, 2. Cf. 'superstitioni enim suae servire cupientes poterunt publice ritum proprium exercere'. *C. Th.* 9, 16, 1. Schultze's comment gives the true meaning of expressions such as these: 'Mit offenbarer Geringschätzung werden hier die welche den "Drang haben, ihrer Superstition Genüge zu thun" an den öffentlichen Ritus verwiesen. Man empfängt den Eindruck als ob der Kaiser sich selbst aus der Zahl derjenigen, welche dieses Bedürfnis fühlen, ausnehme und die Freiheit der öffentlichen Haruspicin im Tone souveräner Verachtung dieser letzteren weiterhin gewährleiste.' Cf. 'qui vero id *vobis existimatis conducere*' in *C. Th.* 9, 16, 2 (A.D. 319), 'retento more veteris observantiae', *C. Th.* 16, 10, 1 (A.D. 320), and 'praeteritae usurpationis officia', *C. Th.* 9, 16, 2; these lead up naturally to the 'aliena superstitio' of *C. Th.* 16, 2, 5 from participation in which the Christians are freed in 323. See V. Schultze, *Untersuchungen zur Geschichte Konstantins d. Gr.*, Zeitschrift für Kirchengeschichte 8 (1886), pp. 520–1.

48. For Philumenos, Optatus, 1, 26 (Ziwsa, p. 28), cf. Athanasius, *Apologia contra Arianos*, 60; Bidez: edition of Philostorgius, p. 10[23]; and see Batiffol, *Bulletin de la Société nationale des Antiquaires de France*, 1914, pp. 209–11, F. Martroye, *ibid.*, pp. 217–20, criticized by Batiffol, *ibid.*, pp. 226–7.

49. Optatus, Ziwsa, p. 28, lines 4–7 'ut remotis duobus unum ordinarent' is the reading of the MSS. with the exception of the Corbie-Petrograd MS. which gives 'remotis binis singulos ord.'; this I cannot translate. The reading of the other MSS. is not easy to understand: I take it to mean that while the two leaders of the parties were kept in custody, the bishops should institute a single head of a united African church. Dr. Turner proposes to read *singula* for *singulos*, retaining *binis* (*Journal of Theological Studies* 27, p. 292), but I am unable to accept his explanation of the bishops' mission.

50. The reading (Ziwsa, p. 28) is doubtful. With Augustine Brev. Coll. 38 I should be inclined to omit *nec*, and read 'Donatus petiit ut ei reverti licuisset et ad Carthaginem accederet'.

51. I have based this chronology upon a study of the documents: these can be found in von Soden's collection (see p. 38), and it is unnecessary to attempt to justify in detail this reconstruction. It will suffice to say (i) that I accept Seeck's emendation of the date of Constantine's letter (Ziwsa, p. 212) to the vicar of Africa, Domitius Celsus (read Martias for Maias), 27 February 316; cf. Seeck, *Regesten*, pp. 142–3; (ii) I think that Seeck's entry under

September 315 (*Regesten*, p. 164)—'Constantin geht von Rom nach Mailand und entscheidet dort den donatistischen Streit'—is an error; this decision was only pronounced in November 316; and (iii) I can see no evidence for Constantine's presence in Milan in November 316, as is stated by Paul Monceaux in his valuable paper *L'église donatiste avant Saint Augustin*, Revue de l'histoire des religions 60 (1909), pp. 1–63, at p. 28. On point (ii) it is to be remarked that, though Augustine in Epist. 43 § 20 writes that Constantine caused the Donatists to be brought to Milan and then, after the arrival of Caecilian, 'ipsum quoque, sicut scripsit, exhibuit, cognitaque causa qua diligentia qua cautela, qua provisione, sicut eius indicant litterae, Caecilianum innocentissimum, illos improbissimos iudicavit', yet, when in the controversy with the Donatists the whole subject of the chronology of the various inquiries is minutely discussed, for the final judgement of Constantine the letter to the vicarius Eumalius is cited, and that letter is dated 'Sabino et Rufino consulibus quarto idus novembres' (Ad. Don. post Coll. 33 § 56); it is incredible that Constantine should have waited for more than a year before acquainting his vicarius of his acquittal of Caecilian.

52. I find it quite impossible to follow Martroye in his contention that Constantine did not himself decide the controversy nor issue, as a result of that decision, a constitution directed against the Donatists. So far as it concerns the action of Constantine I think that his paper—F. Martroye, *La répression du Donatisme et la politique religieuse de Constantin et de ses successeurs en Afrique*, Mémoires de la Société nationale des Antiquaires de France, 8me Série, 3me Tome, 1913 (published 1914), pp. 23–140—is misconceived.

53. Was the persecution of Licinius according to the account of Eusebius directed against Christians in the army, or those of the civil service? It has generally been concluded that Eusebius refers to the army and not to the militarily organized civil service which was itself a *militia* although *inermis*. I doubt this. The language of Eusebius is remarkable: *H.E.* x. 8, 10, εἶτα δὲ τοὺς κατὰ πόλιν στρατιώτας ἐκκρίνεσθαι καὶ ἀποβάλλεσθαι τοῦ τῆς τιμῆς ἀξιώματος εἰ μὴ τοῖς δαίμοσιν θύειν αἱροῖντο παρακελεύεται which becomes in *V.C.* i. 54, τοὺς κατὰ πόλιν στρατιώτας ἡγεμονικῶν ταγμάτων ἀποβάλλεσθαι κ.τ.λ. (as in *H.E.*). ἐγυμνοῦντο δῆτα τῶν κατὰ πᾶν ἔθνος ἀξιωμάτων αἱ τάξεις ἀνδρῶν θεοσεβῶν. In the first place note the peculiar phrase used by Eusebius in both places τοὺς κατὰ πόλιν στρατιώτας; it was long ago suggested by Neander that the words

mean that the measure was limited in its application to the capital Nicomedia (cf. Görres, *Kritische Untersuchungen über die Licinianische Christenverfolgung*, Jena, 1875, pp. 41 f.); but the 'purification' of the *court* of Licinius had previously taken place, and it is difficult to think that beyond the soldiers immediately attached to the court there was any large standing garrison in Nicomedia. I would suggest that the term is carefully chosen to define the *civil* militia—the members of the *militia inermis*. This interpretation is, I think, supported by a consideration of Eusebian linguistic usage, for these στρατιῶται are further defined as belonging to the ἡγεμονικὰ τάγματα. With this phrase, cf. *V.C.* iii. 26, Heikel, p. 90¹¹ οὐδείς τε τῶν πώποτε οὐχ ἡγουμένων, οὐ στρατηγῶν, οὐκ αὐτῶν βασιλέων, ἐπὶ καθαιρέσει τῶν τετολμημένων (= the measures against the Christians) εὕρηται ἐπιτήδειος ἢ μόνος εἷς ὁ τῷ παμβασιλεῖ θεῷ φίλος. The contrast is clear: ἡγούμενοι here = civil governors, στρατηγοί = military commanders. With this passage compare the Eusebian translation of the letter of Constantine in which the emperor orders the restoration or construction of churches αἰτήσειε δὲ καὶ αὐτὸς καὶ διὰ σοῦ οἱ λοιποὶ τὰ ἀναγκαῖα παρά τε τῶν ἡγεμονευόντων καὶ τῆς ἐπαρχικῆς τάξεως (Heikel, p. 61⁵), i.e. you will ask for the necessary means for this work from the *praesides* and from the *officium* of the provincial governor (for ἔπαρχος and ἐπαρχικός see Heikel's Index). Eusebius regularly employs the term ἔθνος for *provincia* (cf. the indexes of Schwartz and Heikel *sub v.*) and in Constantine's decree of restoration after the defeat of Licinius the emperor orders that restoration shall be made to all ὅσοι τοῦ μὴ εἰδωλολατρῆσαι χάριν ὑπὸ τῶν κατ' ἔθνος ἡγουμένων ἐξορίας καὶ μετοικίας ὑπέμειναν (Heikel, 49¹⁴). The κατ' ἔθνος ἡγούμενοι are surely not as Heikel suggests in his Index the *duces*, but the *praesides* who must have acted as judges in the trial of the Christians. Similarly the τὰ κατὰ πᾶν ἔθνος ἀξιώματα of *V.C.* i, 54, of which the Christians were deprived are, I would suggest, the offices in the *civil* hierarchy of the provincial service.

This result of a consideration of Eusebian linguistic usage is strengthened by reference to the wording of the inscription of Eugenius where the term ἡγεμονικὴ τάξις surely = the *officium* of the provincial governor. [So Franchi de' Cavalieri and Batiffol, *Bulletin d'ancienne littérature et d'archéologie chrétiennes* 1 (1911), pp. 25–34, as against Calder; for the bibliography of studies of the inscription, cf. *Journal of Roman Studies* 10 (1920), p. 42, n. 2.] Further for the use of the term τοὺς κατὰ πόλιν στρατιώτας with reference to the *militia inermis*, cf. Batiffol's article on the term στρατεία as = the imperial *civil* service in *Bulletin de la Société nationale des Antiquaires de France*, 1911, pp. 226–32. I do not know of any clear proof that the 'persecution' extended to the army; the Passion of the Forty Martyrs of Sebaste is of ambiguous historicity, and as a document suspect; the Testament of the Martyrs which is probably genuine in no wise suggests, as Franchi de' Cavalieri has shown, that the martyrs were soldiers. The 'martyrdom' of S. Theagenes is of course not relevant to the point at issue, since he was punished for refusal to serve in the army. Licinius needed all his armed forces to meet Constantine, the unconquered general, in the coming struggle, and though he might try to secure the loyalty of the Danubian sun-worshippers in his army by a solemn profession of his belief in the cult of the Deus Sanctus Sol, this as little carries with it of necessity a persecution of his Christian soldiers as did the same cult when practised by Constantius Chlorus.[1]

54. For date, cf. N. H. Baynes, *Journal of Roman Studies* 18 (1928), pp. 218–20; Ernst Gerland, *In Welchem Jahre gelangte Konstantin der Grosse zur Alleinherrschaft?* Byzantinische Zeitschrift 30 (1929–30), pp. 364–73, where the bibliography of recent work on the subject will be found. For an account of the military operations written with knowledge of the country see Sir Edwin Pears, *The Campaign against Paganism*, English Historical Review 24 (1909), pp. 1–17.

55. The important fact to recognize is that Constantine is here not thinking only of the persecution of Licinius—many of the modern accounts of the persecution of Licinius are, in my judgement, erroneous, because based upon this presupposition—but rather of the whole period of the persecutions. It is a comprehensive measure designed to put an end once and for all to the wrongs which the Christians of the eastern provinces had suffered during the past twenty years. The character of the document has been rightly comprehended by Antonio Casamassa in his able paper *I documenti della 'Vita Constantini' di Eusebio Cesareense* published in Letture Costantiniane, Desclée, Roma, 1914, pp. 1–60.

56. In 1898 Crivellucci, arguing that the document was a Eusebian forgery, wrote of this passage 'Il Dio adorato da Cos-

---

[1] For the inscription of Sulsovia (rediscovered in 1903) probably to be dated to A.D. 322 (cf. Parvan: *Sulsovia*, pp. 27 sqq., Bukarest, 1906) see Raymund Netzhammer: *Die christlichen Altertümer der Dobrudscha*, Bukarest, 1918, pp. 19 sqq. The text runs:
'Dei Sancti Solis simulacrum consecratum die XIIII Kalendas Decembres. Debet singulis annis iusso sacro Dominorum nostrorum Licini Augusti et Licini Caesaris ture cereis et profusionibus eodem die a praeposito et vexillatione in castris Sulsoviensibus agentibus exorari. Valerius Romulus vir perfectissimus dux, secutus iussionem, describsit.

tanzo o era il Dio dei cristiani ed egli poteva essere considerato come cristiano o non era, e sarebbe stato affatto indifferente che egli fosse monoteista; per un cristiano egli sarebbe stato sempre un empio, un ateo. Qual passo dunque o vuol dire che Costanzo era cristiano o non ha senso'. *Studi Storici* 7, pp. 453–9 at p. 454. This is to forget that the writer of this passage had been, like his father, a solar monotheist and that it was through solar monotheism that he had come to Christianity (see further pp. 95–103 *infra*). For the pagan monotheism of the period, cf. P. Batiffol, *Summus Deus* = Excursus B in his book *La Paix constantinienne et le Catholicisme*, Lecoffre, Paris, 1914, pp. 188–201, reprinted from the *Bulletin d'ancienne littérature et d'archéologie chrétiennes* 3 (1913), pp. 132–41.

57. V. Gardthausen writes of Constantine: 'Er liebte den Zick-zackkurs; wenn er in einem Jahre untrügliche Beweise seines christlichen Glaubens gegeben, so folgten in den nächsten Jahren ebenso untrügliche Beweise des Gegenteils'. *Das alte Monogramm*, Hiersemann, Leipzig, 1924, p. 75. The purpose of this lecture is to suggest that this is a false conclusion, that the religious policy of Constantine is a continuous approximation, as circumstances permitted, towards a goal which Constantine had clearly determined; in a word that Mariano is right in his contention that the emperor's consistent aim was the triumph of Christianity and the union of the Roman state with the Christian Church. 'Onde, se non è proprio lui stesso che fa del cristianesimo l'unica religione di stato, è pur lui che, con deliberato proposito e tenace coerenza, lo avvia a diventarlo, e predispone le condizioni necessarie, perchè lo diventi definitivamente e immancabilmente.' Raffaele Mariano, *Nuova Antologia* (see p. 38), 1890, at p. 286.

58. An example of the application by Constantine of the toleration proclaimed in this edict is given by the inscription of Nikagoras the priest of the Eleusinian mysteries. Having visited the Tombs of the Kings at Thebes (Egypt) Nikagoras in a *graffito* recorded his presence: ὁ δᾳδοῦχος τῶν ἁγιοτάτων Ἐλευσινίων μυστηρίων [Νικαγόρας] Μινουκιανοῦ Ἀθηναῖος, ἱστορήσας τὰς σύριγγας, πολλοῖς ὕστερον χρόνοις μετὰ τὸν θεῖον Πλάτωνα ἀπὸ τῶν Ἀθηνῶν ἐθαύμασα καὶ χάριν ἔσχον τοῖς θεοῖς καὶ τῷ εὐσεβεστάτῳ βασιλεῖ Κωνσταντίνῳ τῷ τοῦτό μοι παρασχόντι. This inscription, as J. Baillet has shown (*Constantin et le dadouque d'Eleusis*, Comptes Rendus, Académie des Inscriptions et Belles Lettres, 1922, pp. 282–96) is dated to the year 326. 'Constantin a dû mettre à la disposition du prêtre d'Éleusis la poste impériale, le *cursus publicus*, comme pour les évêques . . . sans doute y a-t-il joint quelques subsides' (p. 287). M. Baillet's

further inferences seem to me, I confess, without adequate foundation.

59. The authenticity of the letter is denied by P. Batiffol, *Les Documents de la Vita Constantini*, Bulletin d'ancienne littérature et d'archéologie chrétiennes 4 (1914), at pp. 83-6. The grounds there given for the contention that the letter is a Semi-Arian forgery seem to me singularly inadequate to support such a conclusion. It must always be remembered that Constantine had only recently arrived in the East, and could as yet have gained little detailed knowledge of the dispute; in his experience of ecclesiastical controversy in the West no dogmatic issue had been raised, and in his writings up to this date the emperor had given but slight evidence of any interest in Christian theology (though the opening paragraphs of his encyclical to the Orientals must not be forgotten). I cannot conceive in whose interest this letter could later have been forged; surely, after Nicaea, no fourth-century Christian, not even Monsignor Batiffol's hypothetical Semi-Arian, could have written in this way of the dogmatic issues raised by Arius. We are constantly reminded that Batiffol did not possess that critical judgement which distinguishes the work of Duchesne.

60. τήν τε θείαν πρόνοιαν καλέσας ἀρωγὸν τῷ πράγματι μέσον τῆς πρὸς ἀλλήλους ὑμῶν ἀμφισβητήσεως οἷον εἰρήνης πρύτανιν ἐμαυτὸν εἰκότως προσάγω Eusebius, *V.C.* 2, 68 (Heikel, p. 68⁹⁻¹¹). οὐκοῦν ἑκάτερος ὑμῶν, ἐξ ἴσου τὴν συγγνώμην παρασχών, ὅπερ ἂν ὑμῖν ὁ συνθεράπων ὑμῶν δικαίως παραινῇ δεξάσθω *ibid.*, c. 69 (Heikel, p. 68, 26–8). ὁ μέγας ἡμῶν θεός, ὁ σωτὴρ ἁπάντων, κοινὸν ἅπασι τὸ φῶς ἐξέτεινεν· ὑφ' οὗ τῇ προνοίᾳ ταύτην ἐμοὶ τῷ θεραπευτῇ τοῦ κρείττονος τὴν σπουδὴν εἰς τέλος ἐνεγκεῖν συγχωρήσατε, ὅπως αὐτοὺς τοὺς ἐκείνου δήμους ἐμῇ προσφωνήσει καὶ ὑπηρεσίᾳ καὶ νουθεσίας ἐνστάσει πρὸς τὴν τῆς συνόδου κοινωνίαν ἐπανάγοιμι. *ibid.*, c. 71 (Heikel, p. 70, 9–14).

61. The Council of Antioch. All discussions of this subject depend upon the paper of Eduard Schwartz, *Zur Geschichte des Athanasius*, vi, Nachrichten (see p. 50), 1905, pp. 271 ff. To this Harnack replied that the letter of a Council of Antioch (preserved in a Syriac translation) published by Schwartz was a forgery: *Die Angebliche Synode von Antiochia im Jahr 324–5*, Sitzungsberichte der Kgl. preussischen Akademie der Wissenschaften, 1908, no. xxvi, pp. 477–91. The rejoinder of Schwartz appeared in *Nachrichten* (see p. 50), 1908—*Zur Geschichte des Athanasius*, vii, pp. 305–74—written unhappily in a mood of embittered scorn. Harnack's answer, under the same title as his former paper, is to be found in *Sitzungsberichte der Kgl. preussischen Akademie der Wissenschaften*, 1909,

xiv, pp. 401–25. F. Nau subsequently republished the Syriac text (including the Canons of the Council) with a French translation; he rejects the hypothesis of a Council of Antioch in 324–5: *Littérature canonique syriaque inédite*, Revue de l'Orient chrétien, 2me Série, T. 4 (1909), pp. 3–31. The opinions of other scholars are reported in Erich Seeberg, *Die Synode von Antiochien im Jahre 324–5. Ein Beitrag zur Geschichte des Konzils von Nicäa* (= Neue Studien zur Geschichte der Theologie und der Kirche, edd. N. Bonwetsch and R. Seeberg, Heft 16), Trowitzsch, Berlin, 1913, pp. 1–3. This is an excellent monograph. D. Lebedev has discussed the question of the Council at length: in 1911 in his paper *Antiokhiiskii sobor 324 goda i ego poslanie k Aleksandru, episkopu thessaloniskomu* in Khristianskoe Chtenie for 1911, July–August, pp. 831–58, September–October, pp. 1008–23; later in a review of Seeberg's book: *Vizantiiskii Vremennik* 19 (1912 really 1915), Otdyel ii, pp. 55–146, and again in his article *K voprosu ob Antiokhiiskom soborye 324 goda i o 'velikom i svyashchennom soborye v Ankirye'*, Trudui imperatorskoi Kievskoi Dukhovnoi Akademii, God lv, Kniga iv (April 1914), pp. 585–601; Kniga vii–viii (July–August 1914), pp. 496–532, Kniga xi (November 1914), pp. 330–60; God lvi, Kniga i (January 1915); pp. 75–117. I believe that he has written further on the subject in the *Bogoslovskii Vyestnik*, but this journal is inaccessible to me. We are not here concerned with the many problems raised by this Syriac text; it is sufficient for our purpose that most scholars agree that the document is genuine. In the *Journal of Roman Studies* 18 (1928), p. 219, I suggested that the summoning of the Council of Ancyra was originally the work of the bishops assembled at the Council of Antioch. Since writing that review, I have found that the suggestion had already been made by A. I. Brilliantov in the second part of his paper *K istorii arianskago spora do pervago vselenkskago sobora* in Khristianskoe Chtenie, October 1913, pp. 1176–1200. I have considered, but am not convinced by, the objections raised by Lebedev, *Vizantiiskii Vremennik* 19 (1912), Otdyel ii, pp. 103 sqq.

62. The Council of Nicaea. There has been published in connexion with the recent celebration of the sixteenth centenary of the Council a large number of papers, many of which are not intended to advance the serious study of the many problems which still await solution. Most of these articles have been noted in the current bibliography of the *Byzantinische Zeitschrift*, see e.g. 26 (1926), pp. 195–6; *ibid.*, pp. 454–5: the references need not be repeated here.

An important study of the sources for the history of the Council was contributed by P. Batiffol, *Les sources de l'histoire du Concile de Nicée*, Échos d'Orient 28 (1925), pp. 385–402, 30 (1927), pp. 5–17. In particular there has been much discussion of the worth of the Church History of Gelasius Bk. ii for a reconstruction of the course of the debates; G. Loeschke with the natural partiality of an editor for his author [1] in his dissertation *Das Syntagma des Gelasius Cyzicenus* [Rheinisches Museum 60 (1905), pp. 594–613, 61 (1906), pp. 34–77, and also separately, Georgi, Bonn, 1906, pp. 71], maintained the historical credibility of the account of Gelasius, and in particular defended the 'Protokollstücke' of a dialogue between the Nicene fathers and an Arian philosopher Phaidon. This view he held to the last—thus in the posthumous work edited by Hans Lietzmann in 1913 he writes: 'besonders der Protokolle Echtheit ist oft und bestimmt bestritten; mir ist sie nach wie vor wahrsheinlich' (G. Loeschke, *Zwei Kirchengeschichtliche Entwürfe*, Mohr, Tübingen, 1913, at pp. 33–4). But this judgement can hardly be supported: 'Das Verhältnis des Gelasius zu seinen Quellen wird neu untersucht werden müssen' wrote Margret Heinemann in the Introduction to the new edition of Gelasius (see below, n. 1); cf. the section *Gelasius, sein Werk und seine Quellen*, ibid., pp. xxviii–xxxviii. For the criticism of Gelasius, cf. F. Haase, *Zur Glaubwürdigkeit des Gelasius von Cyzicus*, Byzantinisch-neugriechische Jahrbücher 1 (1920), pp. 90–93, and see his book *Die koptischen Quellen zum Konzil von Nicäa* (= Studien zur Geschichte und Kultur des Altertums, edd. E. Drerup, H. Grimme and J. P. Kirsch, Bd. 10, Heft 4), Schöningh, Paderborn, 1920, sub voc. *Gelasius* in Index; M. Jugie, *La dispute des philosophes païens avec les Pères de Nicée*, Échos d'Orient 28 (1925), pp. 403–10; P. Batiffol, *Échos d'Orient* 30 (1927), pp. 14–16. But in my judgement the Constantinian documents inserted in the work of Gelasius stand upon another footing, and I believe these to be genuine. For an attempt to defend one of the most disputed of these documents see my *Athanasiana*, Journal of Egyptian Archaeology 11 (1925), at pp. 61–5.

Our accounts of the Council are lamentably insufficient; they do but raise problems which are perhaps insoluble. These difficulties are often minimized (cf. C. A. Bernouilli, *Das Konzil von Nicäa*, Mohr, Freiburg and Leipzig, 1896). 'The numbers, character, and composition of the Council are matters on which we have sufficient but not absolute information' (B. J. Kidd,

---

[1] *Gelasius Kirchengeschichte herausgegeben auf Grund der nachgelassenen Papiere von Prof. Lic. Gerhard Loeschke durch Dr. Margret Heinemann*, Hinrichs, Leipzig, 1918 (= Die griechischen christlichen Schriftsteller, vol. 28).

A History of the Church to A.D. *461*, Clarendon Press, Oxford, vol. 2, 1922, p. 23). A historical student can only wonder at the ease with which a theologian can be satisfied. It is very doubtful whether there ever existed any official report of the proceedings. A. Wikenhauser thinks it probable that imperial stenographers were present (*Zur Frage nach der Existenz von nizänischen Synodalprotokollen* in Konstantin der Grosse und seine Zeit—see p. 51—pp. 122–42), but at most it is only a probability—'Ein Verhandlungsprotokoll der Synode hat es wahrscheinlich nie gegeben' (Loofs). The source of the all-important word ὁμοούσιος—who suggested it?—is unknown. The word is perhaps of eastern—and not western—origin, see Ed. Schwartz, *Kaiser Constantin und die christliche Kirche* (see p. 33), pp. 138–42; it still seems to me possible that the Council simply affirmed what Arius had denied. It is very difficult to say in what precise sense the Council understood the word: '*allein* das Schlagwort ὁμοούσιος über den Sinn des Nicänums nicht aufklären kann. Es muss untersucht werden in welchem Sinne und innerhalb welcher Gedankenkreise der Terminus vor Nicäa und bald nachher angewendet wurde. Danach erst kann die Frage erörtert werden, wie und in Zusammenhang mit welchen andern Vorstellungen man in Nicäa das ὁμοούσιος verstand' (F. Loofs, *Das Nicänum* in the Festgabe für Karl Müller, Mohr, Tübingen, 1922, pp. 68–82, and separately). As Schwartz has shown, the ambiguity of the term served Constantine's purpose; he desired no further definition of the creed; its acceptance sufficed. On the term, cf. Engelbert Krebs, ʿΟμοούσιος. *Eine dogmengeschichtliche Darstellung zum 1600 Jahrestag des Nicänums* in Hochland, 22 (1924–5), 257–77.

Of recent works on the Council the best study known to me is that of A. E. Burn, *The Council of Nicaea. A memorial for its sixteenth centenary*, S.P.C.K., London, 1925; cf. further A. d'Alès, *Le Dogme de Nicée*, Beauchesne, Paris, 1926; for a paper written from the standpoint of the Orthodox Church, cf. Joannes Phokulides, ʿΗ ἐν Νικαίᾳ πρώτη Οἰκουμενικὴ Σύνοδος in ʾΕκκλησιαστικὸς Φάρος 24 (1925), pp. 133–244. There is still room in my judgement for a full critical monograph upon the Council by one who should be both a student of history and of theology.

Of the numerous problems one only need be noticed here: the question of the presidency of the Council. This has always been a disputed point and Dom Leclercq terminates his discussion with the words: 'La question demeure douteuse et n'apercevant pas l'utilité d'une affirmation prématurée nous nous abstiendrons de prendre parti.' C. J. Hefele, *Histoire des Conciles, I*, Part 1, Paris, 1907, pp. 425–7 where references are given. Cf. V. Grumel, *Le siège de Rome et le Concile de Nicée. Convocation et présidence*, Échos d'Orient 28 (1925), pp. 411–23 (who refers to J. Devillard, *La Papauté et le Concile de Nicée*, Revue Apologétique 40, pp. 400 sqq. which I have not seen), and C. A. Kneller, *Das Papsttum auf dem ersten Konzil von Nicäa*, Stimmen aus Maria-Laach 77 (1909), pp. 503–22. Harnack, to explain contradictions in our authorities, has suggested that the bishops of the more important sees presided in turn. The point, however, from which consideration of the question should start is, in my judgement, the meaning of the phrase of Eusebius, *V.C.* iii. 13 Constantine παρεδίδου τὸν λόγον τοῖς τῆς συνόδου προέδροις. That phrase is generally taken in the sense that after his speech the emperor vacated the chair and handed over the presidency to the πρόεδροι: so in the fullest discussion of the passage known to me, that of P. Wolff, *Die πρόεδροι auf der Synode zu Nicäa*, Zeitschrift für kirchliche Wissenschaft und kirchliches Leben 10 (1889), pp. 137–51, who decides, it would appear to me, arbitrarily, that there were precisely *two* πρόεδροι—Eustathius and Alexander of Alexandria. But it has long been recognized that the procedure of the early Christian Councils was based upon that of the Roman senate: cf. in particular P. Batiffol, *Le règlement des premiers conciles africains et le règlement du sénat romain*, Bulletin d'ancienne littérature et d'archéologie chrétiennes 3 (1913), pp. 3–19; *id.*, *Origines de règlement des conciles* in Pierre Batiffol, Études de liturgie et d'archéologie chrétienne, Lecoffre and Picard, Paris, 1919, pp. 84–153; cf. H. Gelzer, *Die Konzilien als Reichsparlamente* in Ausgewählte kleine Schriften, Teubner, Leipzig, 1907, pp. 142–55. After the *relatio* of the consul, the leading senators in turn are asked their opinion (sententiam rogare, sententiam dicere). Surely the Eusebian account supposes the same procedure: Constantine makes his *relatio* in Latin, this is translated into Greek, and thereupon he asks the opinion of the leading bishops—he gave them the opportunity of speaking. ἐντεῦθεν δὲ οἱ μὲν ἀρξάμενοι κατηγιῶντο τοὺς πέλας, οἱ δ'ἀπελογοῦντό τε καὶ ἀντεμέμφοντο. In such an atmosphere Constantine did well to retain the presidency of the Council; only thus could he successfully guide its decisions.

63. For the action taken by the Council in the case of Eusebius of Nicomedia and Theognis of Nicaea, cf. Ed. Schwartz, *Zur Geschichte des Athanasius*, viii, Nachrichten (see p. 50), 1911, Heft 4, pp. 380–4, and the discussion by K. Müller of Anhang i and Anhang ii of G. Loeschke and M. Heinemann's edition of Gelasius Cyzicenus (= pp. 192 ff. and p. 200) in his *Kleine Beiträge zur alten*

Kirchengeschichte, No. 13. *Zu der Eingabe der Bischöfe Euseb von Nikomedien und Theognis von Nicaea an die [zweite] Synode von Nicaea [327]*, Zeitschrift für die neutestamentliche Wissenschaft &c., 24 (1925), pp. 278–92, at pp. 290–2.

64. This letter is devoted to the subject of the date of the celebration of Easter, now fixed for the whole church by the Council: that date will be independent of calculations made by the Jews, those parricides and slayers of their Lord. It is indeed scandalous that without the aid of the Jews the Christians cannot celebrate their Easter feast. The letter stands in the list of Semi-Arian forgeries which Batiffol thought that he could discern in the *Vita Constantini*. It would serve no useful purpose to consider Batiffol's grounds for his view in each individual case (see p. 42), but it may be worth while to discuss the reasons adduced for his conclusion in a single instance. (i) Constantine speaks of the rule concerning Easter which 'we have followed from the beginning'. 'Un évêque peut parler ainsi qui par la succession apostolique se rattache aux apôtres, mais un empereur qui n'est pas même catéchumène, qui n'a donc jamais encore célébré la fête pascale!' But throughout his letters Constantine identifies himself with the Christians—from the day when in A.D. 314 he wrote 'deus noster'. (ii) 'Whatever', writes Constantine, 'has been done in the holy councils of bishops, this should be attributed to the divine will' (Gel. Cyz., p. 133, 11–13). 'Maxime épiscopale plutôt qu'impériale' comments Batiffol. Yet in 314 Constantine in his letter to the bishops assembled at Arles had written 'dico enim, ut se veritas habet, sacerdotum iudicium ita debet haberi ac si ipse dominus residens iudicet'. (iii) The letter is an episcopal sermon, continues Batiffol; 'ce n'est surtout pas dans ces invectives contre les Juifs le langage d'un empereur et moins encore de l'empereur Constantin qui a été bienveillant pour les Juifs.' Yet in his constitutions concerning the Jews Constantine speaks of their religion as a 'feralis secta' (*C. Th.* 16, 8, 1) and a 'nefaria secta', and orders that any one who attacks a convert from Judaism to Christianity shall be burnt alive, while he forbids conversions to Judaism. It is true that he exempts from personal *munera* the Jewish priests, but this is only to confirm a traditional exemption (cf. Juster, *Les Juifs dans l'Empire romain*, Geuthner, Paris, 1914, vol. 1, p. 408). When Batiffol writes of a rescript of 11 December 321, that by it 'l'exemption des charges de la curie est accordée à perpétuité' he forgets to mention that this rescript abolishes the privilege of exemption from the decurionate. 'Pourtant *ad solacium pristinae observationis* il maintint l'ancienne dispense pour

deux ou trois fonctionnaires, seulement, de la communauté juive' (Juster, *op. cit.*, vol. 2, p. 259). And for any one considering the dispositions of *Sirm.* 4 it might not appear easy to hold that Constantine 'a été bienveillant pour les Juifs'. (iv) Finally Batiffol writes that the letter supposes that the decree of the Council had met with some resistance and is intended to disarm this opposition. This is, he thinks, the position in which the Council of Antioch of the year 341 found itself. But was there no resistance to be feared after Nicaea? Cf. Burn, *The Council of Nicaea*, S.P.C.K., London, 1925, pp. 37–9 on 'the compact of silence' at the Council.

It is not with arguments such as these that the letters of Constantine can be proved to be forgeries.

65. See Schwartz, *Zur Geschichte des Athanasius*, viii, Nachrichten (see p. 50), 1911, pp. 367–426.

66. One of the greatest services which Otto Seeck rendered to students of the history of the Council of Nicaea was, in my judgement, to point out that the Council was summoned for a second session in the year 327. His famous article *Untersuchungen zur Geschichte des Nicänischen Konzils*, Zeitschrift für Kirchengeschichte 17 (1896), pp. 1–71, 319–62 was marred by so much hypercriticism that it seems to-day to be forgotten by some writers, as e.g. by K. Müller, *Zeitschrift für die neutestamentliche Wissenschaft* &c. 24 (1925), p. 290. Ed. Schwartz has accepted (without acknowledgement) the fact of this second session of the Council, *Zur Geschichte des Athanasius* viii (see note 65), and in this I believe him to be right. I have not yet been able to see a recent criticism of Seeck's view by B. K. Stephanides, Ἡ ἐκ δευτέρου τῷ 327 σύγκλησις τῆς ἐν Νικαίᾳ Α΄ Οἰκουμενικῆς Συνόδου *(325)*, Ἐπετηρὶς Ἑταιρείας Βυζαντινῶν Σπουδῶν 6 (1929), pp. 45–53.

67. Cf. Gelasius Cyzicenus, edd. Loeschke and Heinemann, p. 163, 30 ff.

68. Cf. H. I. Bell, *Jews and Christians in Egypt*, &c., British Museum, 1924, pp. 45–71; id., *Athanasius: A chapter in church history*, The Congregational Quarterly 3 (1925), pp. 158–76.

69. For the views expressed in these paragraphs, cf. N. H. Baynes, *Athanasiana*, Journal of Egyptian Archaeology 11 (1925), pp. 58–69, at pp. 61–5; id., *Journal of Roman Studies* 18 (1928), pp. 220–1; id., *Alexandria and Constantinople: a study in ecclesiastical diplomacy*, Journal of Egyptian Archaeology 12 (1926), pp. 145–56.

70. For the interpretation of the words (Eusebius, *V.C.* 4, 24) attributed to Constantine ἀλλ᾽ ὑμεῖς (the bishops) μὲν τῶν εἴσω τῆς

ἐκκλησίας, ἐγὼ δὲ τῶν ἐκτὸς ὑπὸ θεοῦ καθεσταμένος ἐπίσκοπος ἂν εἴην (ed. Heikel, p. 126, 9–11), cf. E. Ch. Babut, *Évêque du dehors*, Revue critique d'histoire et de littérature N.S. 68 (1909), pp. 362–4. For the personal meaning—οἱ ἐκτός—cf. 1 *Cor.* 5, 13; *Col.*, 4, 5; 1 *Thess.*, 4, 12; Athanasius, *Apol. c. Ar.*, 3 τῶν ἔξω τις. The translation of Valesius gave currency to the phrase 'évêque du dehors': 'le succès durable de son erreur prouve une fois de plus que les auteurs grecs se lisent beaucoup en latin.' The term may be regarded as the Christian rendering of the pagan title Pontifex Maximus; for the retention of the latter title by Christian sovereigns, cf. *Bulletin de la Société nationale des Antiquaires de France*, 1928, pp. 192–7; it cannot be traced, as was once thought, in the sixth century, cf. Zeiller, *ibid.*, pp. 174–7. For the title Pontifex —often inclitus, but not Maximus—borne by Christian sovereigns in the fifth and sixth centuries, cf. Batiffol, *ibid.*, 1926, pp. 223–27 (this usage is not found after Justinian). For the difficulties which the fact of Constantine's retention of the pagan title cause to the Roman Catholic apologist, cf. A. Bernareggi, *Costantino Imperatore e Pontefice massimo. Casistica storica*, La Scuola cattolica, Anno 41, Serie 5, vol. 2 (1913), pp. 237–53.

71. Batiffol objects: Why is there no mention in the letter of Donatists or Melitians? The answer is surely simple: the Donatists had been left to the judgement of Heaven; the Melitians had been reconciled at the Council of Nicaea. The article in *La Civiltà cattolica*, Ann. 58 (1907), vol. 2, pp. 660–72 on *Le eresie e la legislazione de' primi imperatori cristiani* is of no value.

72. For these passages, cf. Gel. Cyz., p. 53, 17 ff., 194–5, 180–1, Athanasius, *Apologia contra Arianos*, 86. The article by E. Krebs, *Die missionsgeschichtliche Bedeutung Konstantins des Grossen*, Zeitschrift für Missionswissenschaft 3 (1913), pp. 177–86 is out of print, and I have been unable to secure a copy.

73. Cf. N. H. Baynes, *Rome and Armenia in the Fourth Century*, English Historical Review 25 (1910), pp. 625–43, at pp. 627–8; *id.*, *Athanasiana*, Journal of Egyptian Archaeology 11 (1925) at pp. 65–7 (with further bibliographical references); *id.*, *Journal of Roman Studies* 18 (1928), at p. 222.

74. Eusebius, *Vita Constantini*, 2, 53. Here, I believe, is to be found the explanation of the enigmatic Armenian war of Maximin.

75. Cf. Gelasius Cyzicenus, p. 128; Eusebius, *V.C.* 3, 66; Adolf Harnack, *Porphyrius*, '*Gegen die Christen*', *15 Bücher. Zeugnisse, Fragmente und Referate.* Einzelausgabe (= Abhandlungen der Königl. preuss. Akademie der Wissenschaften, Jahrgang 1916, Phil.-hist.

Klasse, Nr. 1), Berlin, 1916, pp. 5, 31 (Zeugnisse, no. ix), 39 (Zeugnisse, no. xxiv. *C.J.* 1, 5, 6; 1, 1, 3). 'Die Verfügung ist das erste staatliche Bücherverbot im Interesse der Kirche.' Harnack, p. 31. See Socrates, *H.E.* 1, 9.

76. No satisfactory treatment of this subject is known to me; Nicolo Marini's paper on *Costantino Magno e l'unione delle chiese*, Bessarione 29 (1913), pp. 217–47, 393–419 is concerned with the reasons for, and the effect of, the foundation of Constantinople.

77. I have briefly outlined my view of the later development in *Some Aspects of Byzantine Civilization*, Journal of Roman Studies 20 (1930), pp. 1–13.

78. In this lecture it is unnecessary to consider the legend of Constantine's baptism at the hands of the Pope; the historical facts are now unquestioned, cf. F. J. Dölger, *Die Taufe Konstantins und ihre Probleme* in Konstantin der Grosse und seine Zeit (see p. 51), pp. 377–447. The origins of the Silvester legend are still in doubt: did it arise in Armenia or Syria? (so Duchesne; Ryssel would say Syria), or in Rome? (so Schaskolsky). 'Es wäre besonders für die Kenntnis der kirchenpolitischen und dogmengeschichtlichen Strömungen ein Vorteil, wenn die Legende auf breitester Grundlage untersucht würde' (Dölger, p. 398 n.). To the bibliographical references for the legend given by Dölger may be added: I. Guidi, *Il battesimo di Costantino imperatore*, Nuova Antologia, 2nda. serie, 41 (1883), 41–52; P. Schaskolsky, *La leggenda di Costantino il Grande e di Papa Silvestro*, Roma e l'Oriente, Anno 3, vol. 6 (1913), pp. 12–25; and Anon., *Il testo greco del βίος di S. Silvestro attribuito al Metafraste* (here published for the first time), *ibid.*, pp. 332–67. In the account of the baptism given by Eusebius the translation of the emperor's words μὴ δὴ οὖν ἀμφιβολία τις γιγνέσθω has given rise to much discussion: Keim rendered them 'es schwinde nun jede Zweideutigkeit' with the comment 'so hat er (Constantine) sterbend der Welt eingestanden dass er ein Leben der Rätsel und Widersprüche hinter sich liess'. *Der Ubertritt Konstantins*, &c. (see p. 34), p. 1. V. Şesan, *Kirche und Staat* &c. (see p. 37), pp. 353–6, translated 'möge nun also jeder Zweifel (*betreffend mein Seelenheil*: ist die einzig mögliche Ergänzung!) schwinden . . . Um die σωτηρία allein ist Konstantin, wie jeder Christ, angesichts des Todes sehr besorgt!' But ἀμφιβολία, there can be little doubt, here = 'hesitation', 'delay': 'dass aber ἀμφιβολία hier "Zaudern" bedeutet, darüber lässt der Zusammenhang keinen Zweifel. Konstantin spricht von einem nunmehr endgiltigen Entschlusse sich sofort taufen zu lassen, während er bisher die Taufe immer

aufgeschoben hat in der Absicht sie einmal im Jordan zu emp-
fangen.' L. Wrzoł, *Konstantins des Grossen persönliche Stellung zum
Christentum* (see p. 37), p. 247, n. 8. This is, I think, the true
interpretation of the words (cf. Dölger, *op. cit.*, pp. 426–9). For
the fourth-century practice of delayed baptism and the reasons
for the delay, cf. L. Wrzoł, *loc. cit.*, and Dölger, pp. 429–37. Ed.
Schwartz's interpretation of Eusebius, *V.C.* 1, 32—that Constantine had previously belonged to the class of the Christian ἀκροώμενοι
—is very doubtful; I should rather agree with those who understand the words αὐτὸς δ' ἤδη τοῖς ἐνθέοις ἀναγνώμασι προσέχειν ἠξίου
to refer to Constantine's private reading of the scriptures. Cf. Ed.
Schwartz, *Zur Geschichte des Athanasius*, Nachrichten (see p. 50),
1904, p. 545; *id.,/Kaiser Constantin und die christliche Kirche* (see
p. 36), p. 68 f.; Dölger, *op. cit.*, pp. 437–40; K. Müller, *Kleine
Beiträge zur alten Kirchengeschichte*, No. 11, Zeitschrift für die
neutestamentliche Wissenschaft, &c. 24 (1925), pp. 285–6. On
the classes amongst the catechumens see Ed. Schwartz, *Bussstufen
und Katechumenatsklassen*, Schriften der Wissenschaftlichen Gesellschaft in Strassburg, Heft 7, Trübner, Strassburg, 1911.

For the funeral of Constantine see the admirable study by
Franchi de' Cavalieri, *I Funerali ed il sepolcro di Costantino Magno*,
Mélanges d'Archéologie et d'Histoire 36 (1916–17), pp. 205–61;
when army and state had paid their tribute, the church received
its champion and celebrated its Christian obsequies. For the
Mausoleum of Constantine see A. Heisenberg, *Grabeskirche und
Apostelkirche*, Teil 2, *Die Apostelkirche in Konstantinopel*, Hin-
richs, Leipzig, 1908 at pp. 106–9; Egger, *Die Begräbnisstätte des
Kaisers Konstantin*, Jahreshefte des österreichischen archäologischen
Institutes 16 (1913), Vienna, pp. 212–30, V. Schultze, *Altchristliche Städte und Landschaften*, 1. *Konstantinopel*, Deichert, Leipzig,
1913, pp. 13–15. For traces of the apotheosis of the emperor, cf.
P. Collomp, Revue de Philologie 36 (1912), pp. 196–201, and
P. Lejay, *L'ascension à travers les cieux dans Eusèbe de Césarée, H.E.* x. 4,
15, *ibid.*, pp. 201–2; and cf. in general, L. Bréhier and P. Batiffol,
Les survivances du culte impérial romain, Picard, Paris, 1920; on
divus, divinus in Christian texts see Martroye, *Bulletin de la Société
nationale des Antiquaires de France*, 1928, pp. 297–9; and see Jules
Maurice, *ibid.*, 1901, pp. 341–2. For 'the thirteenth Apostle' as
possible successor of 'the thirteenth God', cf. Otto Weinreich,
Triskaidekadische Studien, Beiträge zur Geschichte der Zahlen (= Reli-
gionsgeschichtliche Versuche und Vorarbeiten, vol. 16, Heft 1),
Töpelmann, Giessen, 1916, at pp. 3–14. The statement of Xan-
thopoulos Nikephoros Kallistos writing in the fourteenth century

of the site of the Mausoleum of Constantine—ὁ βωμὸς ʽΕλλήνων
πρότερον ἦν, δωδεκάθεον ὄνομα, θέαμα λόγου πολλοῦ ἄξιον, Migne,
P.G. 146, col. 220 c—is otherwise unsupported, and seems a frail
basis for the theory. Constantine had ever felt himself, as 'man
of God', to have a mission entrusted to him; he would be buried in
the mausoleum attached to the Church of the twelve missionaries
of God which was unfinished at the emperor's death. Christian
hymnody in recalling the parallel of S. Paul was in fact faithfully
reflecting Constantine's own thought. For this parallel, cf. the
Menaeum quoted by Weinreich, *op. cit.*, p. 8:

> οὐκ ἐξ ἀνθρώπων τὴν κλῆσιν ἔλαβες
> ἀλλ' ὡς ὁ θεσπέσιος Παῦλος
> ἔσχες μᾶλλον, ἔνδοξε, ταύτην
> ἐξ ὕψους, Κωνσταντῖνε ἰσαπόστολε.

See A. Baumstark, *Konstantiniana aus syrischer Kunst und Liturgie*,
No. 3. *Konstantin der 'Apostelgleiche' und das Kirchengesangbuch des
Severus von Antiocheia*, in Konstantin der Grosse und seine Zeit
(see p. 51), pp. 248–54. For the view of the Orthodox Church
to-day Weinreich refers to A. von Maltzew, *Menologien der orthod.-
kath. Kirche des Morgenlandes*, Berlin, 1901, vol. 2, pp. 335–6. The
words of Eusebius (*V.C.* 4, 60) τῆς τῶν ἀποστόλων προσρήσεως
κοινωνὸν τὸ ἑαυτοῦ σκῆνος μετὰ θάνατον προνοῶν ὑπερβαλλούσῃ πίστεως
προθυμίᾳ γενήσεσθαι are understood by V. Schultze in the sense
'dass in der Fülle der Gebete welche die Zwölfzahl der Apostel
anregen musste, auch des Heils seiner Seele als des Erbauers und
dort Schlummernden gedacht werde'. *Altchristliche Städte*, &c. (see
supra), p. 14. I think the meaning to be, rather, in view of what
follows—ὡς ἂν καὶ μετὰ τελευτὴν ἀξιῶτο τῶν ἐνταυθοῖ μελλουσῶν ἐπὶ
τιμῇ τῶν ἀποστόλων συντελεῖσθαι εὐχῶν—that he, as an apostle, might
share with the apostles in the prayers which were addressed to
them: cf. c. 71: καὶ τοῦ σπουδασθέντος αὐτῷ τόπου σὺν τῇ τῶν ἀποστόλων κατηξιοῦτο μνήμῃ, ὡς ὁρᾶν ⟨ἔστι⟩ εἰσέτι καὶ νῦν τὸ μὲν τῆς τρισ-
μακαρίας ψυχῆς σκῆνος τῷ τῶν ἀποστόλων προσρήματι συνδοξαζόμενον
—'même après sa mort on vénérera dans sa personne la protection
divine qu'il a reçue et qui lui a permis de triompher des ennemis du
christianisme' (Bréhier and Batiffol, *op. cit.*, pp. 41–2). A. Heisenberg would go further than this—'der *divus imperator* der den
christlichen Staat gegründet, wollte gegraben und nach seinem
Tode verehrt sein nicht anders als der Sohn Gottes, der die christliche Religion gegründet hatte' (*op. cit.*, pp. 115–16). In this I cannot
follow him. Constantine takes his place in a church dedicated
to the Apostles; the fact that both the Church of the Holy Sepulchre

and the Church of the Twelve Apostles were built on a similar architectural plan does not of itself justify the inference that Constantine desired to occupy in the worship of his Mausoleum the same position as Christ took as of right in the 'Grabeskirche' of Jerusalem. Beyond this architectural similarity I know of no evidence which would support Heisenberg's view.

APPENDIX

For the student of the religious policy pursued by Constantine the crucial period is that which lies between the Battle of the Milvian Bridge and the Battle of Chrysopolis. From a study of the actions, and more particularly of the letters, of Constantine I feel convinced that there was no attempt made by the emperor during this period to found a new syncretistic religion[1]; I cannot believe that Constantine's own thought was at this time consciously syncretistic:[2] he regarded himself definitely as a Christian, and that point I have endeavoured to illustrate in my lecture. But if this is so, what account are we to give of the 'two religions' which have been brought into clear relief by the studies of M. Maurice (cf. in particular his articles *Les discours des Panegyrici Latini et l'évolution religieuse sous le règne de Constantin*, Comptes Rendus, Académie des Inscriptions et Belles Lettres, 1909, pp. 165–79, and *L'origine des seconds Flaviens, ibid.*, 1910, pp. 96–103 at pp. 101–3), how are we to explain the continuance down to 323 of the Sol invictus types on the coinage? Certain considerations readily suggest themselves. In the first place Constantine still shared the rule of the empire with a colleague. Licinius had accepted the religious policy of Constantine at the famous meeting at Milan early in 313, but there is no evidence that Licinius himself was ever enthusiastic in the maintenance of that policy, and Constantine might well be reluctant to force the pace in the matter of a coinage which, though issued by one ruler, was intended for use within the whole empire. Only after 323 was Constantine free to determine imperial policy alike in East and West. Further, we may lay stress upon the fact that the officials of the imperial Moneta were doubtless at this time mainly pagan, and we may recognize fully with Maurice[3] the large independence of action which such officials enjoyed. But this independence would hardly extend to the determination of the character of such a magnificent

---

[1] Cf. e.g. Theodor Zahn, see p. 34 *supra*.   [2] Cf. e.g. Salvatorelli.

[3] Cf. his *Numismatique Constantinienne, passim*; and see *Bulletin de la Société des Antiquaires de France*, 1901, pp. 197–201.

medallion as that published by Babelon [1] which was in all probability intended to commemorate the meeting of Constantine and Licinius at Milan. Here the Sol Invictus type must surely have been dictated by the emperor's personal choice. I cannot but feel that at times Maurice is inclined to assign to the influence of the pagan officials of the imperial mint a greater weight than can be reasonably attributed to it when we consider the personality of Constantine and the boldness of his masterful initiative.

There is, however, a third explanation to which, in my judgement, scholars have tended to pay insufficient attention. Since Constantine had abandoned his early title to the throne and had openly disclaimed his Herculian inheritance, Sol Invictus had become, as it were, the heraldic device of the dynasty of the Second Flavians. Through this solar worship Constantine was most closely and obviously associated with his heroic ancestor Claudius Gothicus. Recent studies of this solar cult of the Flavian house [2] have enabled us to see more clearly its significance and vitality. Licinius could base his title to empire upon the choice of Galerius, the legitimate representative of the Jovian dynasty; Constantine in A.D. 312 had defeated the unworthy son of the Herculian Maximian, it was essential for him now that he had severed the links which bound him to the 'Successionsordnung' of Diocletian to establish in the minds of his new subjects his true title to the purple—no mere *pronunciamento* of the army, but an inheritance which stretched behind the reorganization of Diocletian, beyond the new-fangled dynasties of Jovians and Herculians, back to the emperor who, like a Roman of the ancient days, had devoted himself to death upon the battlefield in the service of the Roman state. There might come a time—one could not tell—when an eastern colleague might challenge his authority to govern the Roman West; the cult of Sol Invictus, if that day came, might serve as the heirloom which should establish his title to that majestic inheritance. The citizens of Termessos in Pisidia remembered that claim in their dedication Κωνσταντείνῳ ⟨νέῳ⟩ Ἡλίῳ παντεπόπτῃ.[3] Dynastic considerations such as these go far to explain Constantine's retention of solar types upon his coinage.

[1] E. Babelon, *Un nouveau médaillon en or de Constantin le Grand*, Mélanges Boissier, Fontemoing, Paris, 1903, pp. 49–55.

[2] See note 24 on p. 57.

[3] Cf. Lancoronski, *Villes de la Pamphylie et de la Pisidie*, Paris, 1893, ii, p. 218, no. 82; F. Cumont, *Textes et Monuments figurés relatifs aux mystères de Mithra*, i, p. 290. See F. J. Dölger, *Sol Salutis. Gebet und Gesang im christlichen Altertum*, &c. = Liturgiegeschichtliche Forschungen, Heft 4–5, Aschendorff, Münster, 1920, p. 55. For the Christian λόγος παντεπόπτης see Dölger, *Die Sonne der Gerechtigkeit*

CONSTANTINE AND THE CHRISTIAN CHURCH   97

And yet I feel that even these considerations do not carry us all the way; for one who holds the view which I have attempted to support in this lecture there still remains a problem. That problem I cannot solve, but I should like to make some tentative suggestions towards its solution. May it not be that the continuance of these solar types should rather be explained from Constantine's own experience and the desire that that experience should in its turn be shared by others? Constantius Chlorus, as we know from his coinage, worshipped the Unconquered Sun [1]; he was a monotheist, in the words of Eusebius (*V.C.* 1, 17) μόνον μὲν θεὸν ἐπιγνοὺς τὸν ἐπὶ πάντων, τῆς δὲ τῶν ἀθέων κατεγνωκὼς πολυθεΐας; that cult Constantine inherited. Let us suppose, for a moment at least, that the emperor was not entirely foresworn when he recounted to Eusebius the story of his vision. Athwart the sun, the earthly representation of the God to whom he owed this inherited allegiance, was cast the cross of light; what else could this mean for Constantine than a revelation of the identity of the God of his worship with the God of the Christians? 'Whom therefore ye ignorantly worship, him declare I unto you.' The secret of his father's monotheism was disclosed. Apollo—Sol—the pagan panegyrist two years before at Trier had celebrated as 'salutifer'; it was true in a sense of which the orator had never dreamt; Constantine will later write ἔσχον ἔγωγε τοὺς πρὸ τούτου γενομένους αὐτοκράτορας διὰ τὸ τῶν τρόπων ἄγριον ἀποσκλήρους, μόνος δ' ὁ πατὴρ ὁ ἐμὸς ἡμερότητος ἔργα μετεχειρίζετο, μετὰ θαυμαστῆς εὐλαβείας ἐν πάσαις ταῖς ἑαυτοῦ πράξεσι τὸν σωτῆρα θεὸν ἐπικαλούμενος.[2] And when Constantine turned to the Christian Church for enlightenment, he would find not a little which would support his identification. How much support he could gain for that view can best be gauged by a careful study of Dölger's *Sol Salutis*.[3] It was to the rising sun that Christians alike in East and West turned in prayer, whether in congregational worship or in private devotion. In Tertullian's day there were already some who thought the sun to be the Christians' God: 'Alii plane humanius solem Christianum deum aestimant, quod innotuerit ad orientis partem facere nos precationem, vel die solis laetitiam curare. Quid vos minus facitis? Non plerique affectatione adorandi aliquando etiam caelestia ad

und der Schwarze (=Liturgiegeschichtliche Forschungen, Heft 2), Aschendorff, Münster, 1918, p. 107, and *Sol Salutis*, p. 108.

[1] For the heliolatry of Constantius Chlorus, cf. *Bulletin de la Société nationale des Antiquaires de France*, 1924, p. 102. Medallion found at Beaurans near Arras with legend 'Reditus lucis aeternae'.

[2] *V.C.* 2, 49. Cf. Batiffol in *Bulletin d'ancienne littérature et d'archéologie chrétiennes* 3 (1913), pp. 179–81.   [3] For full title see p. 96, n. 3.

solis initium labra vibratis?'¹ The same misconception is discussed by Tertullian in the Apologeticum, c. 16.² It is relevant
to note the recent discussion of the precise significance of the solar
iconography on the Roman coins. On this Usener writes: 'Der
Sonnengott mit Strahlenkrone geschmückt, nackt bis auf die
über die linke Schulter zum Rücken herabfallende Chlamys,
plegft nach links gewandt zu stehen oder zu schreiten, auf das
rechte Bein gestüzt; die rechte Hand mit ausgestreckten Fin-
gern ist wie zum Segnen erhoben, die linke trägt entweder die
Peitsche oder die Weltkugel . . . Die Peitsche in der Hand des
Gottes lässt darauf schliessen, dass in erster Linie eine Darstellung
des von seinem Viergespann dahingetragen Sonnengottes berück-
sichtigt wurde, wie sie in Rom zB. auf dem Tempelgiebel des
Apollo Palatinus angebracht war. Die Weltkugel werden wir
uns in der Hand des Tempelbildes zu denken haben, das für alle
uns beschäftigenden Münzbilder maassgebend wurde.'³ On this
Dölger comments: 'Usener hat in dem Namen [Sol Invictus]
allzusehr die Allmacht des Sonnengottes erkennen wollen [cf.
Usener, *op. cit.*, pp. 468 ff.]. Dies lag aber in der Verkennung
mancher Bilder... Beim Gestus der erhobenen Rechten spricht nun
Usener von "segnender rechter Hand". Die richtige Deutung gibt
uns aus antikem Vorstellungskreis Prokopius in seiner Beschreibung
der Kunstuhr von Gaza. Von der beweglichen Figur des Helios,
die an den 12 Stundentüren (zur Öffnung) vorüberzieht, heisst
es: "Seine Linke hält die Himmelskugel empor, die Rechte streckt
er aus um den Befehl zum Öffnen der (Stunden-) Türen zu geben,
wie man den Pferden das Zeichen zum Verlassen der Schranken
gibt."⁴ Im christlichen Kampf mit dem Sonnenkult wurde da-
gegen stark betont, dass die Sonne nicht selbsttätig wirke, sondern
von Christus, dem Schöpfer der Sonne, abhängig sei. So wird es
begreiflich dass Christus im Gestus des Sonnengottes erscheint.
Nach dem Bartholomäusevangelium streckt Christus am Morgen

---

¹ Tertullian, *Ad nationes* 1, 13 (J. G. P. Borleffs, *Ad Nationes*, Brill, Leiden,
1929, p. 26, 13 ff.).
² See the edition of the Apologeticum of J. E. B. Mayor and A. Souter,
Cambridge University Press, 1917, p. 54, and notes thereon pp. 255–6.
³ H. Usener, *Sol Invictus*, Rheinisches Museum N.F. 60 (1905), p. 470. 'Dies
Bild ist eine Schöpfung hellenistischer Kunst und gehört einer anderen Welt
an als der Fetisch von Emesa', *ibid.*, p. 471. The history of the solar coinage of
the Roman Empire down to the Constantinian period is given by Usener in
this paper, pp. 469–80.
⁴ H. Diels, *Über die von Prokop beschriebene Kunstuhr von Gaza*, Abhandlungen
der K. Preuss. Akad. d. Wiss., Jahrg. 1917, Phil.-hist. Klasse, No. 7, Berlin,
1917, p. 33.

die Hand aus und gibt damit der Sonne den Befehl zum Aufgang.
So ist nun auch der Gestus des Sonnengottes auf dem Viergespann
zu verstehen, da der Sonnengott als aufgehende durch das Sonnen-
tor des Ostens gehende Sonne gedacht ist . . . Sol invictus ist die
von der Finsternis nicht bezwungene und zum Zeichen des Sieges
morgens wieder auftauchende Sonne.'[1] It is this resurrection of
the sun from the prison of the dark which is signified by the word
Oriens on the Roman coinage.[2] From this we see that the Christian
parallel is very close. The Church early identified Christ with the
Sun of Righteousness which should arise with healing in his wings
(Malachi 4, 2)[3]; this identification appears in Clemens of Alexandria.[4] Philo had already interpreted Zach. 6, 12 'See a man
whose name is ἀνατολή' (cf. Oriens), as 'See a man whose name is
Sunrise', and four times in Justin's dialogue with Trypho this
passage is quoted and Ἀνατολή is referred to Christ.[5] As Kloster-
man has suggested, in the words of Luke 1, 78–9:

$$\delta\iota\grave{\alpha}\ \sigma\pi\lambda\acute{\alpha}\gamma\chi\nu\alpha\ \acute{\epsilon}\lambda\acute{\epsilon}ous\ \theta\epsilon o\hat{v}\ \acute{\eta}\mu\hat{\omega}\nu$$
$$\acute{\epsilon}\nu\ o\acute{\iota}s\ \acute{\epsilon}\pi\iota\sigma\kappa\acute{\epsilon}\psi\epsilon\tau\alpha\iota\ \acute{\eta}\mu\hat{\alpha}s\ \acute{\alpha}\nu\alpha\tauo\lambda\grave{\eta}\ \acute{\epsilon}\xi\ \acute{v}\psi ous$$
$$\acute{\epsilon}\pi\iota\phi\hat{\alpha}\nu\alpha\iota\ \tauo\hat{\iota}s\ \acute{\epsilon}\nu\ \sigma\kappa\acute{o}\tau\epsilon\iota\ \kappa\alpha\grave{\iota}\ \sigma\kappa\iota\hat{q}\ \theta\alpha\nu\acute{\alpha}\tauou\ \kappa\alpha\theta\eta\mu\acute{\epsilon}\nuo\iota s$$
$$\tauo\hat{v}\ \kappa\alpha\tau\epsilon v\theta\hat{v}\nu\alpha\iota\ \tauo\grave{v}s\ \pi\acute{o}\delta\alpha s\ \acute{\eta}\mu\hat{\omega}\nu\ \epsilon\acute{\iota}s\ \acute{o}\delta\grave{o}\nu\ \epsilon\acute{\iota}\rho\acute{\eta}\nu\eta s$$

ἀνατολή is not merely 'der Vorgang des Aufgehens', 'sondern das
Gestirn selbst als Bild für den Messias'.[6] Ἀνατολή ist dann genau
wie das lateinische Oriens sowohl der Osten als die aufgehende
Sonne.'[7] Just as the Unconquered Sun rises in glory and cannot
be holden of the dark so we read in Melito of Sardis:

$$\beta\alpha\sigma\iota\lambda\epsilon\grave{v}s\ o\acute{v}\rho\alpha\nu\hat{\omega}\nu,$$
$$\kappa\alpha\grave{\iota}\ \kappa\tau\acute{\iota}\sigma\epsilon\omega s\ \acute{\eta}\gamma\epsilon\mu\acute{\omega}\nu,$$
$$\H{\eta}\lambda\iota os\ \acute{\alpha}\nu\alpha\tauo\lambda\hat{\eta}s$$
$$\H{o}s\ \kappa\alpha\grave{\iota}\ \tauo\hat{\iota}s\ \acute{\epsilon}\nu\ \H{q}\delta ou\ \nu\epsilon\kappa\rho o\hat{\iota}s\ \acute{\epsilon}\phi\acute{\alpha}\nu\eta$$
$$\kappa\alpha\grave{\iota}\ \tauo\hat{\iota}s\ \acute{\epsilon}\nu\ \kappa\acute{o}\sigma\mu\omega\ \beta\rho o\tauo\hat{\iota}s,$$
$$\kappa\alpha\grave{\iota}\ \mu\acute{o}\nu os\ \H{\eta}\lambda\iota os\ o\hat{v}\tau os$$
$$\acute{\alpha}\nu\acute{\epsilon}\tau\epsilon\iota\lambda\epsilon\nu\ \acute{\epsilon}\xi\ o\acute{v}\rho\alpha\nuo\hat{v},[8]$$

[1] F. J. Dölger, *Sol Salutis* (see p. 96), pp. 289–90.

[2] H. Usener, *op. cit.*, pp. 471 ff.

[3] F. J. Dölger, *Die Sonne der Gerechtigkeit und der Schwarze. Eine religions-
geschichtliche Studie zum Taufgelöbnis* (= Liturgiegeschichtliche Forschungen,
Heft 2), Aschendorff, Münster, 1918, especially at pp. 100–10.

[4] F. J. Dölger, *Sol Salutis* (see p. 96, n. 3), p. 108.

[5] Dölger, *ibid.*, pp. 109–15.

[6] E. Klostermann, *Handbuch zum N.T.*, vol. 2, pt. 1, Tübingen, 1919, p. 389
(cited by Dölger).   [7] Dölger, *ibid.*, p. 114.

[8] Melito of Sardis περὶ λουτροῦ, 4. 'Die poesievolle Sprache kommt durch
die Gliederung zum Ausdruck'. Dölger, *ibid.*, p. 115, n. 1.

so in Clemens of Alexandria

$$\text{'}E\gamma\epsilon\iota\rho\epsilon \ \acute{o} \ \kappa\alpha\theta\epsilon\acute{\upsilon}\delta\omega\nu$$
$$\kappa\alpha\grave{\iota} \ \acute{a}\nu\acute{a}\sigma\tau\alpha \ \acute{\epsilon}\kappa \ \tau\hat{\omega}\nu \ \nu\epsilon\kappa\rho\hat{\omega}\nu,$$
$$\kappa\alpha\grave{\iota} \ \acute{\epsilon}\pi\iota\phi\alpha\acute{\upsilon}\sigma\epsilon\iota \ \sigma\iota \ \acute{o} \ X\rho\iota\sigma\tau\grave{o}s \ \kappa\acute{\upsilon}\rho\iota\sigma s,$$
$$\acute{o} \ \tau\hat{\eta}s \ \acute{a}\nu\alpha\sigma\tau\acute{a}\sigma\epsilon\omega s \ \mathring{\eta}\lambda\iota\sigma s,$$
$$\acute{o} \ \pi\rho\grave{o} \ \acute{\epsilon}\omega\sigma\phi\acute{o}\rho\sigma\upsilon \ \gamma\epsilon\nu\nu\acute{\omega}\mu\epsilon\nu\sigma s,$$
$$\acute{o} \ \zeta\omega\grave{\eta}\nu \ \chi\alpha\rho\iota\sigma\acute{a}\mu\epsilon\nu\sigma s \ \acute{a}\kappa\tau\hat{\iota}\sigma\iota\nu \ \acute{\iota}\delta\acute{\iota}\alpha\iota s.\text{[1]}$$

We are accustomed to think of Constantine's use of the term *dies solis* as purely pagan, but would it have offended fourth-century Christians? Thus Jerome in an Easter sermon on the text 'This is the day which the Lord hath made; we will rejoice and be glad in it' (Ps. 118, 24) can say, 'The Lord indeed made all days; other days can be claimed by Jews, heretics, and pagans. The day of the Lord, the day of resurrection, the Christians' day is our day. And it is called the day of the Lord because on this day the Lord rose victorious to the presence of the Father. When the pagans call it the day of the Sun we welcome the name, for to-day the Light of the World has arisen, to-day the Sun of Righteousness has arisen with healing in his wings.'[2] Maximus of Turin speaking of the festal period from Easter to Whitsun can go further in one of his sermons: 'Sicut dominica solemus facere, erecti et feriati resurrectionem Domini celebramus. Dominica cuius nobis ideo venerabilis est atque solemnis, quia in ea salvator, velut sol oriens, discussis inferorum tenebris, luce resurrectionis emicuit, ac propterea ipsa dies ab hominibus saeculi dies solis vocatur, quod ortus eam sol iustitiae Christus illuminet.'[3] I cannot think that bishops at the Western court, willing to smooth Constantine's path, would have proved themselves less generous.

And 'Sol invictus'? What better description for the Victorious Christ? 'In einer Sammlung lateinischer Übersetzungen von Predigten des Johannes Chrysostomos', writes Usener, 'hat sich eine Schrift über die Heiligung der vier Jahrpunkte erhalten, die bei der Gestaltung des christlichen Festkalenders eine bedeutsame Rolle gespielt hat. Ihr Verfasser, ein aus bäuerlichen Verhältnissen hervorgegangener romischer Kleriker, sucht den gefähr-

---

[1] 'Klemens führt diesen Text so an, als ob die sechs Glieder ein zusammenhängendes Ganze bilden sollten'; Protrept., 8, 84, 1-2. Dölger, *ibid.*, pp. 282-3.

[2] *Anecdota Maredsolana*, iii. 2 (1897), p. 418. (Dölger, *ibid.*, p. 286.) 'Dies dominica, dies resurrectionis, dies Xpistianorum, dies nostra est. Unde et dominica dicitur: quia Dominus in ea victor ascendit ad Patrem. Quod si a gentibus dies solis vocatur et nos hoc libentissime confitemur: hodie enim lux mundi orta est, hodie sol iustitiae ortus est, in cuius pennis est sanitas.

[3] Migne, *P.L.* 57, 371 (Dölger, *ibid.*, p. 287).

lichsten Einwand, den ebenso Heiden wie strengere Christen gegen die kirchliche Weihnachtsfeier erheben konnten, mit folgendem Trumpf abzuweisen: "Aber man nennt den Tag auch Geburtsfest des *Invictus*. Ja wer ist denn so unbesiegbar ausser unserem Herrn, der den Tod siegreich unterworfen hat?"'[1] On 25 December 'the new sun' was born:[2] the birthday of the Sol Invictus was popularly known as 'Sol Novus'. 'Bene quodammodo', says Maximus of Turin (if the sermon is rightly attributed to him), 'sanctum hunc diem natalis Domini solem novum vulgus appellat, et tanta id sui auctoritate confirmat ut Judaei etiam atque Gentiles in hac voce consentiant. Quod libenter nobis amplectendum est quia oriente Salvatore non solum humani generis salus, sed etiam solis ipsius claritas innovatur. . . . Si enim obscuratur sol, cum Christus patitur, necesse est, illum splendidius solito lucere, cum nascitur.' On this day the sunrise comes before its time. 'Ex eo denique factum puto ut nox decresceret, dum sol festinus ob dominicae nativitatis obsequium ante mundo lucem protulit quam nox cursum sui temporis consumaret. . . . Nec mirari debemus quod in nativitate Christi nova omnia facta sint; cum novum hoc ipsum fuerit quod virgo peperit. . . . Sol igitur praeter consuetudinem in hac festivitate matutinus illuxit; nec mirum: si enim ad Jesu Nave orationem defixus stetit in die, cur non ad Jesu Christi nativitatem festinus promoveret in noctem. Solem igitur novum hanc diem vulgus appellat.' The old sun is the sun of this world, the new sun 'quem nisi Christum Dominum reperimus de quo scriptum est: Orietur vobis sol iustitiae. . . . Sol noster novus . . . deo oritur auctore'.

This suggests an interesting contrast. In Pisidia Constantine is himself hailed as 'the new sun',[3] in Constantinople we are told the colossal statue of Constantine with its radiate crown, facing towards the rising sun *(ἀνθήλιος)*, bore the inscription Κωνσταντίνῳ λάμποντι Ἡλίου δίκην: the emperor is not the God, he looks towards the sun's rising, and in that light reflects the sun's splendour.[4] Under Probus for the first time we meet with the numismatic legend, 'Soli invicto comiti Augusti', which brings into clear relief 'die enge Beziehung des Gottesbegriffs zum Kaiser'.[5] Did

---

[1] Usener, *op. cit.*, pp. 465–6.

[2] Usener, *ibid.*, p. 481; Maximus of Turin, pp. 403–4 of the Roman edition of his works.

[3] On this see note on p. 96; νέῳ is, it must be remembered, a hypothetical insertion.

[4] On this statue and its inscription, cf. Th. Preger, *Konstantinos-Helios*, Hermes 36 (1901), pp. 457–69, especially at pp. 462–3.

[5] 'Eine in ihrer Art einzige Illustration dazu liefern Münzen, auf deren

Constantine 'the man of God' see in this term the natural expression of his relation to the Sun of Righteousness? 'Statt des Gottes der sichtbaren Sonne schenkte Constantin nun seine Verehrung dem Gotte, der die Sonne geschaffen.' Sol iustitiae: 'es ist als ob man die 'Sonne der Gerechtigkeit' gerade für Constantin gesucht und gefunden hätte. An dem sieghaften Zauberwort haben sich die Prediger des IV und V Jh. förmlich berauscht.' [1]

In this solar apologetic of the period I am inclined to see the influence of Constantine; the worship of the Unconquered Sun of paganism may have formed for many the bridge by which they passed into the Christian Church: this would help to explain the Christian worship of the sun in Egypt, and the Christian worship of the sun in Rome against which Eusebius of Alexandria and Pope Leo the Great protested. [2]

From the coinage of Constantine the personal pagan deities—Jupiter, Mars—disappeared, but the symbolic figure of the Unconquered Sun remained. It is not uninteresting to note that Eusebius was, it would seem, prepared to admit in Christian art symbolic figures, such as the Good Shepherd, but refused to allow the legitimacy of personal representations, whether of Christ or of the Apostles: these fell under the ban of Exodus 20, 4. [3] In modern studies of the development of early Christian art I have not noticed any reference to the curious account given in the Passion of the Quattor Coronati. The Christian Pannonian stone-masons carved for Diocletian a colossal statue of the Sun, but when ordered to produce a similar statue of Aesculapius they refused, justifying that refusal by quoting Psalm 115, 8. [4] No explanation is given for their earlier compliance with the imperial command, but it would seem to be most easily explained from the attitude of Eusebius towards symbolic representations. The figure of the

Vorderseite des Brustbild des *Sol* mit Peitsche dem Bild des Kaisers zur Seite gestellt wird [Cohen vi. 282, 300], einmal geradezu als *Sol comes Probi Aug.*' Usener, *op. cit.*, p. 476.   [1] Usener, *ibid.*, p. 480.

[2] Eusebius of Alexandria, περὶ ἀστρονόμων, Migne, *P.G.* 86, 1, 453 C–D (Dölger, *ibid.*, p. 52); Leo the Great, In Nativitate Domini 7, 4, Migne, *P.L.*, 54, 218 f. Dölger, *ibid.*, pp. 1–14. Cf. the quotation from a Syrian scholiast to Bar Salibi (Assemani, *Bibl. orient.* 2, 164) quoted by Usener, *op. cit.*, p. 466.

[3] Walter Elliger, *Die Stellung der alten Christen zu den Bildern in den ersten vier Jahrhunderten* = Studien über christliche Denkmäler, ed. Johannes Ficker, Heft 20, Dieterich, Leipzig, 1930, pp. 50–1.

[4] Previous publications of the text of the Passion have been superseded by the edition of H. Delehaye in the *Acta Sanctorum Novembris*, T. 3, Brussels, 1910, pp. 748–84. On the genuine character of the Pannonian passion as contrasted with later elements in the text of the Acta, cf. *ibid.*, pp. 759–60. Psalm 115, 8, quoted at p. 774.

Unconquered Sun was, it would appear, regarded as a symbol and therefore innocuous. This may throw a side-light upon Constantine's retention upon his coinage of solar types.[1]

The explanation here offered I cannot prove; but for one who like myself cannot accept the view that after 312 Constantine sought to inaugurate a new monotheistic syncretism, the imperial coinage presents a problem which cannot be ignored. In this period Constantine was forced to take account of a colleague who had not passed through his own personal experience, and consequently did not share his convictions. If he was unable to adopt definitely Christian types for his coinage, he could at least make use of the symbolism of a cult through which he had himself been led to Christianity in the hope that others would find the same pathway to Christian truth.

ADDENDUM

July 1931. I desire to add a reference to a few studies which were overlooked by me or have been published since these notes were sent to the press:

With note 16, p. 33, cf. G. Bardy, *La politique religieuse de Constantin après le concile de Nicée*, Revue des Sciences religieuses 8 (1928), pp. 516–51; H. Grégoire, *La 'conversion' de Constantin*, Revue de l'Université de Bruxelles 36 (1931), pp. 231–72 (extract from a forthcoming book *Constantin, l'Histoire et la Légende*); Max Vogelstein, *Kaiseridee-Romidee und das Verhältnis von Staat und Kirche seit Constantin* (=Historische Untersuchungen, ed. E. Kornemann, Heft 7), Marcus, Breslau, 1930, Teil 2, *Constantin und das Christentum*, pp. 50–98.

With note 25, p. 57, cf. W. Weber, *Die Vereinheitlichung der religiösen Welt* in Probleme der Spätantike, Vorträge . . ., gehalten von R. Laqueur, H. Koch, und W. W., Kohlhammer, Stuttgart, 1930, pp. 67–100.

With note 33, p. 60, cf. the article *Labarum* by H. Leclercq in Dict. d'archéologie chrétienne et de liturgie, T. 8, part 1, coll. 927–62.

---

[1] This question of the symbolic character of Constantine's coinage and the extent of that symbolism must be left to the numismatists. Grisar's hint, *Zeitschrift für katholische Theologie* 6 (1862), pp. 597–602, has not been followed up. Alföldi writes to me from Budapest: 'Wir haben Konstantin jetzt als christlichen Heracles auf einer Bronzerelief aus Pannonien.'

With note 36, p. 66, cf. G. Costa, *Mitopeia Costantiniana*, Bilychnis 33 (1929), pp. 283–8.

With note 58, p. 83, cf. P. Graindor, *Constantin et le dadouque Nicagoras*, Byzantion 3 (1926, published 1927), pp. 209-14.

In the bibliography on p. 70 I find that I have by an oversight omitted to mention W. Schnyder, *Die Anerkennung der christlichen Kirche von seiten des römischen Staates unter Konstantin dem Grossen* in Jahres-Bericht der kant. höheren Lehranstalten, der Kunstgewerbeschule und der Fortbildungs-schule für technisches Zeichnen in Luzern für das Schuljahr 1912–13, J. Schills Erben, Luzern, 1913, pp. 69–105. The reference to Schnyder on p. 73 *supra* is to p. 96 of this study.

INDEX

PRINTED IN GREAT BRITAIN
AT THE UNIVERSITY PRESS, OXFORD
BY VIVIAN RIDLER
PRINTER TO THE UNIVERSITY